BREEDING
A PUP OR TWO

BREEDING
A PUP OR TWO

SECOND ADDITION

THOMAS P. DWYER

iUniverse, Inc.
Bloomington

Breeding a Pup or Two
Second Addition

iUniverse books may be ordered through booksellers or by contacting:

iUniverse
1663 Liberty Drive
Bloomington, IN 47403
www.iuniverse.com
1-800-Authors (1-800-288-4677)

ISBN: 978-1-4759-1138-1 (sc)
ISBN: 978-1-4759-1139-8 (hc)
ISBN: 978-1-4759-1140-4 (ebk)

Printed in the United States of America

iUniverse rev. date: 07/23/2012

CONTENTS

Introduction..xi

Chapter 1. Selection...1

Thin Lines: 2
Field Trials Vs. Shows: 2
Training: 8
Breeders: 9
A.K.C: 9
Money: 10
Pet Shops: 10
Colors And Markings: 11
Puppy Prices: 13
Co-Ownership: 13
The Lease: 14
Breeding Dogs: 14
Mixed Breed Vs. Purebred: 15
Unregistered Purebred: 16
Limited Registration: 16
Choosing A Veterinarian: 17
Bedding: 18

Chapter 2. Genetics..23

Complementing: 24
Inbreeding: 25
Line Breeding: 26
Outbreeding: 26
Crossbreeding: 26
Dna Testing: 26
Dna Samples: 27

O.F.A. & Pennhip: 27

Elbows: 29

Eyes: 30

Osteochondritis Dessicans: 30

Cancer: 31

Cryptorchidism: 32

Mange: 34

Chapter 3. Non-Genetics **37**

Blood Work: 37

Heart Murmur: 38

Giardiasis: 39

Brucellosis: 39

Chocolate: 40

Worms: 40

Hypertrophic Osteodystrophy: 42

Lyme Disease Shots: 43

Neutering The Dog: 44

Chapter 4. Mating **47**

Stud Arrangements: 47

Season: 49

Odd Seasons: 50

Split Season: 50

Mating: 51

First Attempt: 52

Second Attempt: 58

Third Attempt: 61

Artificial Insemination: 63

Chapter 5. Maturation **67**

Gestation: 67

Chapter 6. Whelping..**79**

Uterine Inertia:.. 88
Fetal Distress:.. 89
Nearing The End:.. 89

Chapter 7. Puppy Care..**93**

Chilled Pups:.. 94
Crushed Pups:.. 94
Weak Or Sick Puppies:.. 99
Eyes:.. 101

Weaning: **102**

Bloat/Blockage: 107
Worming:.. 108
Diarrhea:.. 108
Acidophilous:.. 109
Calcium:.. 109
Adult Dog Food:.. 110
Opening The Whelping Box: 111
Urinary Track Infections:.. 114
Limping Pups:.. 118
Swimmers.. 119
Pink Eye:.. 119
Final Thoughts:.. 122

In Memory of my mother

Maria G. Dwyer

Daisy

Photo by Tom Dwyer

INTRODUCTION

Have you ever heard the story about the Arab and his camel? If not, then it goes something like this: it seems an Arab had set up camp in the desert and was inside his tent preparing to go to sleep when his camel, who was lying just outside the doorway, began to petition. "Master," he begged, "The desert night is so cold. I wonder if you would allow me to put my head inside of your tent. It would be of great benefit to me." The Arab agreed. Shortly thereafter, the camel again asked if he could also bring one shoulder into the tent. Again, the Arab consented. Eventually, the camel managed to gain access for all of his other parts and ended up in complete possession of the tent's comforts—leaving the Arab outside to deal with the cold desert night.

After having bred many generations of German Shorthaired Pointers and trained scores of others, our house and surrounding property has become home to five adult dogs. How did this happen? Pretty much the same way that the camel got into the tent. It happened over several years: first, there was simply a pet or two around the house; then, slowly but surely, as my commitment to breeding and training increased, the number grew like Topsey. Fortunately, marriage and family life is a never ending series of adjustments and my wife has recently pointed out two separate but related truths regarding our private universe:

1. The camel appears to have his head and both shoulders inside our tent.
2. She is never going to sleep in the desert.

Such is the delicate pitfall of breeding dogs (or any animal for that matter). As one's intensity and level of commitment increases, so might the size of one's animal kingdom. It all starts innocently enough—you simply obtain one dog for the purpose of breeding. If it's a male, you have the best of the economics of breeding and less of the time management problems. If it's the more profitable female, however, be prepared to serve as the midwife who is on call for at least four months at a time.

On the other hand, you may wish to become one of the less than 25% of all dog owners who possess more than one dog. Such being the case, you are once again confronted by the choice of sexes. Depending on your earlier experiences, you could elect to have two males or two females. On the other hand, you may be content with your line quality and simply elect one male and one female. This selection can broaden the possibilities for both economics and opportunity. In my opinion, this is probably the best platform upon which to become an authoritative breeder, but be ready to roll up your sleeves. Not only does this do away with losing the pick of the litter, but it also means that as sole owner of any offspring that is produced, you have complete control and responsibility of the terms of the sale.

As for those 25% of all dog owners who elect to own two dogs, you should know that only 25% of them ever move on to three. Add to the fact that one half of the dogs in that population has been altered, (can't be bred) it means that only a tiny minority are ever acquired by professional breeders. In these cases, selection is an important decision. Two males for example might become extremely combative when a bitch goes into season. Having three males and no females would eliminate the seasonal combat, however, but it could still foster aggressive competitive among them.

Many breeders move on to four or more dogs in order to out-cross, and stagger the breeding as the dogs age. This will insure that they control the breeding lines along with the resulting genealogy. Consequently, the wise breeder will have dogs of varying ages in his kennel. This assures him of three things:

A. He knows the history and life cycle of each of his dogs.
B. Having organized their history and lines, he can plan future breedings accordingly.
C. He now has the advantage of insuring high quality breeding lines in both sires and dams.

Having four dogs also introduces several other considerations. Although doubling up your dogs can be a short-term resolution for housing, bitches that are in season will soon need separate quarters and males, as stated earlier, could quarrel when the bitch is in bloom. By this time the cost of food, shots, and shelter as well as tasks such as grooming, training, and proper pooper scooping will have quadrupled, and you may want to see an analyst to determine what wretched deed in your past brought on this tendency for self destruction.

My personal commitment to the profession of breeding ends with five dogs. More than that would strain my facilities to the breaking point—to say nothing of my wife's dislike for sleeping in the desert. Most important, the good breeder with the proper number of dogs will maintain the health and fitness of his animals throughout their entire life. Whatever your number is, it should be tempered by one of the most infectious dilemmas in the breeding world—how many animals will you be able to provide quality lives for after their breeding days are over?

Here is LeAnna Dwyer handling two German Shorthaired Pointers.
Penny, age eight, is a retired breeding bitch. Behind LeAnna is a
four year old bitch named Patty, who is expecting her first litter.
Photo by Tom Dwyer

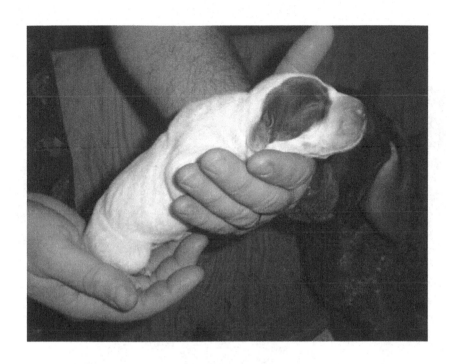

Penny's last litter.
Photos by Jane Dwyer

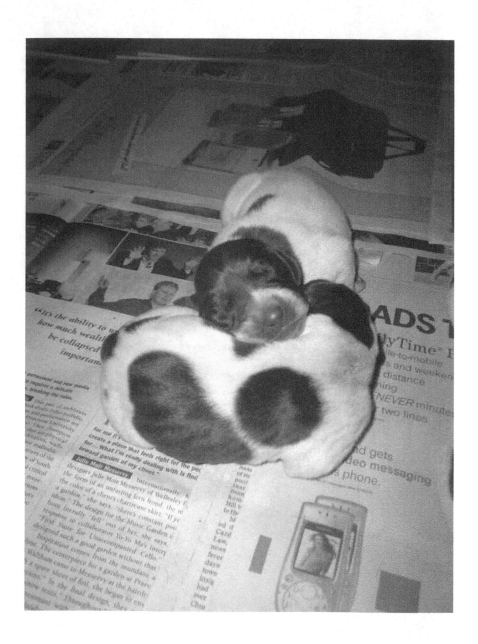

1

Selection

Writing a "how to" book on breeding is like teaching an unseasoned lumberjack how to cut down a tree. The rookies just can't wait to start chipping away at a tree trunk but the problem is that the freshly minted lumberjack still needs someone to teach him how to pick up and hold the ax correctly. Breeding is a little more complex. How much background does the reader already have? Not knowing that, we must assume that no background exists to tell the reader how to pick up and hold the ax. Once we know that however, we can safely have a grasp of where to start the book. Therefore, much of what follows in this chapter will be a brief summary of my first book, *Pointers: Just a Few.* What we will review will be some important details regarding the selection and training of dogs, as well as some basic breeding considerations.

To begin with, purchasing a dog for breeding is not really that different from purchasing a dog for any other reason. Each person wants to believe that they obtained the best dog available for their purpose. Whether the purchase was for protection, fieldwork, show, or just plain companionship, purchasing a dog for breeding should not be any different. There will be no guarantee on the breeding ability of any animal for some time, so, relax and enjoy the process of researching and buying your dog. Worry about the breeding later.

Once you bring a dog into your home, it will probably remain there for a very long time. In light of this, the intensity of your search for that perfect dog should be right up there along side your other major lifetime acquisitions. Most people begin the process having a fair idea of precisely what type of dog they want but frequently get tired of looking, and end up settling for an animal they perceive as *close enough*. Very often this is because the weary buyer ultimately caves into the seller's sweet talk. How many times have I heard the lament; "He looked so cute that I just had

1

to take him home." Another of my personal favorites is, "I got him really cheap." Well, unfortunately *cute* works for only about three weeks, and you should not be looking for bargains for such an important investment; so, here are a few other things you might want to consider before you actually start breeding.

THIN LINES:

Over the years, some breeds have had a very hard time retaining the skills for which they were bred. It seems that every time a certain breed becomes popular, the prospect of owning one begins to work against the basic factors and traits that got the animal to the top in the first place. What happens is that demand exceeds supply and some breeders will begin to use substandard mating in order to fill their demand. This, of course, will result in diluting the quality of the breed and leaving it with severely weakened characteristics. Remember that Dalmatian movie? While searching for your perfect dog, make sure that the line is strong.

FIELD TRIALS VS. SHOWS:

Have you ever compared the physical characteristics of a hunting dog that was bred for field trials to another of the same breed who was bred to compete in the show ring? On the surface, that might be a strange question. If both dogs are the same breed and come from quality stock, how could they be physically different? It is a fact, however, that the science of breeding has always focused on complimenting dames and sires with matching characteristics to insure the extension of those specific traits in the litter. In the case of animals bred for show instead of field trials, those attributes are subtle but indeed different.

On the one hand, show dogs are bred to the highest standards of their kennel organization and are entered into competition in order to determine which will be recognized as the "Best of Breed." Field dogs, conversely, are bred to perform herding or hunting tasks as efficiently as possible. They compete in trials or tests in order to determine which dog can accomplish those tasks best. It is this distinction that is behind the fine-tuning which occurs within the different breeding groups. Although both types of dogs exist within the standards of the breed, they may well be physically different. For example, many field dogs are more muscular and show more ribs than their counterparts in the show arena. While this is desirable for the field dog, it is definitely a liability for show. This also explains why there are fewer dogs that are Dual Champions (winners of championships in both areas of competition). I suspect that it is only a matter of time before many breeds will become permanently subdivided. A case in point would be the Red & White Setter and Irish Setter. Although the purist might reasonably argue against this, I feel that professional breeding achieves its purpose only when it produces dogs who are most suitable to the task at hand and in these cases, we have two clearly different tasks.

There is one common agenda when it comes to both the field and show dogs, and is specifically portrayed by breeders who just have to *have* a title on that particular dog. Obviously the better dog, when entered, should come out on top. However, sometimes dogs will only be entered into a competition where the certain preference of a judge only favors one specific style of dog. In other words, this dog only looks good to a select few and not the majority. While these particular dogs are indeed titled, they can however, be severely handicapped for breeding. Most, but not all breeders, will sell these dogs under a leased or co-owned agreement. There is also a lot of marketing involved.

Tal Allen with Thor
Photo is a self portrait.

Field dogs, conversely, are bred to perform herding or hunting tasks as efficiently as possible. They compete in trials or tests in order to determine which dog can accomplish those tasks best.

Millbrook's Apach-He
Photo By Tom Dwyer

Cedarbay's Mousse-Man Cometh
Photo by Marianne Rousseau

Show dogs are bred to the highest standards of their kennel organization and are entered into competition in order to determine which will be recognized as the "Best of Breed."

Birdland's Barroness Sydney with Chris Holiday
Judge is Marianne Rousseau.
Photo By Tal Allen

**Tom White with Rita and Saddles, who are part of the
infamous Spotted Hill GSP's.
Photo by Tom Dwyer**

**Dual Champions are winners of championships
in both areas of competition.**

Wayne Robinson with Red & White Setters, Robi Lee Sky Walker,
Robi Lee Evening Star & Robi Lee Sky Hawk.
Photo by Lee Robinson

I suspect that it is only a matter of time before many breeds
will become permanently subdivided. A case in point would
be the Red and White Setter and the Irish Setter.

Anna Jones with Dalriach Alchemy.
Photo by Lee Robinson

TRAINING:

Obviously, your dog is going to have to receive some training. A well-trained dog has the potential to influence many succeeding generations. Training brings out the dog's ability as well as demonstrates his intelligence. This is probably the reason why people title their dogs, show strong potential in the breeding pool. Proper training not only accentuates the dog's achievement, but also makes his lines desirable to other breeders.

Evan Dwyer with Miss Elle and Daisy.
Photo by Tom Dwyer

Pat Russell and Tom Dwyer with Birdlands Rudy of the Valley,
Birdlands Mojo, and Millbrooks Double Bogey.
Photo by Tal Alan.

With this in mind, you should know the difference between a *dog that was well trained* and *a smart dog.* Some trainers can do extraordinary things with dogs. One example of this would be the simple *sit* command. A good trainer can teach every single animal he works with to sit and to do it well. Similarly, a good handler can teach a dog to look good while in motion. Both will produce a dog that is well trained. Smart dogs, on the other hand, are guided rather than taught, and will eventually, anticipate your command. I would further submit that by proper selection, this level of intelligence can be bred into the line. To the casual observer, well-trained dogs and smart dogs may appear to function in the same manner; nevertheless, the challenges and training difficulties are at opposite ends of the spectrum. It is also true that all titled dogs are not equally intelligent within any given line, while others rise well above the norm. To the layperson, making this distinction is not always easy.

No matter why you originally bought the dog, he will eventually have to receive some form of training and it follows that if your dog is not properly trained, then it might be more difficult to have him or her bred.

BREEDERS:

Probably the best way to find a reputable breeder is simply to ask a few owners, trainers, or veterinarians for their recommendation. Given the likelihood that you will breed, it would be wise to listen carefully to their advice. Many good breeders also advertise in the pet section of your local newspaper so, that's as good a place as any to begin puppy shopping. If that does not work, expand your search to include the Internet, as well as out of town, statewide, and regional papers. Many breeders are also listed in dog magazines but get your checkbook ready; they could prove to be expensive. There may also be local dog clubs in your area that can help. Nationally, there is an excellent resource: kennel clubs.

A.K.C:

Most folks think of the American Kennel Club as merely a place to register their newest acquisition. Consequently, they buy a dog, mail in some paperwork, and then forget that the organization exists. In point of fact, the AKC has a wealth of information. They have data on almost anything concerning purebred dogs that you would want to know. In addition, they can help you find breed clubs who will in turn, let you know about the availability of a new litter. All you have to do is contact them.

MONEY:

Most quality show and field dogs will fetch top dollar. That does not mean, however, that there are not some quality dogs selling for reasonable prices in the marketplace. Many fine dogs never make it into the ring because their breeders can't afford the competition expenses. This means that there are some excellent canines available to buyers who are focusing on quality. On the other hand, there are breeders who are only trying to squeeze a dollar from a litter whose Dam never should have been bred in the first place. You will recognize them as the breeders who try to talk you into something that you do not want.

PET SHOPS:

Most pet shops are a great place to pick up leashes, food, books, tidbits and fish but if you want to buy a puppy there, I would caution you to think again. I have always fancied the thought that I could turn a quick buck by picking up some puppies and setting them out in a cardboard box on a busy street corner. The problem with this scenario is that like most reputable breeders, I care whom I am selling the dog to and what happens to them in their new home. Similarly, when folks see that doggie in the pet shop window, they probably think what a cute pet he would make. They have an overwhelming urge to take him home because he will be so much better off in their nice warm home than in a small cramped crate. Well, that's part of the hook and sometimes it even comes with a pedigree. It is your choice if you are thinking about buying a pet shop dog. My theory is that I am yet to know a quality breeder who sells quality dogs' to pet shops: hence, it is likely that low-end breeders unload their animals there. In truth, a pet shop's only mission is to sell you a dog—any dog!

Colors And Markings:

All too often, the color and marking of the puppy are the determining factors in your decision making process. Whereas cosmetic appearance is indeed important, it should not cloud your judgment when you weigh it in with all of the other traits that you are looking for. You may find that little puppy birthmark irresistible but be certain that you are comfortable with all of the other markings and colors. The dog will retain his hue for a very long time.

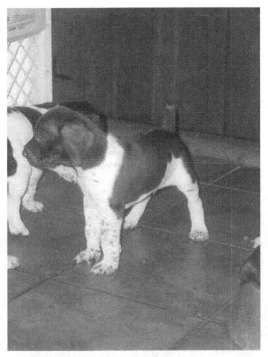

**Birdlands Mojo at six weeks of age.
Photo by Pat Russell.**

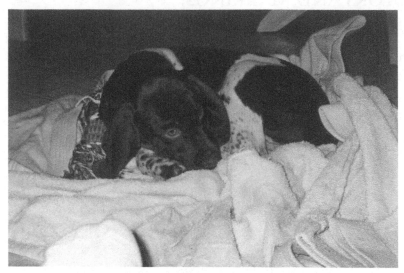

Here is Mojo once again at eight weeks of age.
Photo by Tom Dwyer.

Birdlands Mojo at three years of age.
Photo by Tom Dwyer.

PUPPY PRICES:

The price you pay for a puppy will vary according to the area where you buy him as well as the quality of the dog itself. For example, large dogs in the city might sell for less because of stiffer leash laws. There may also be a breeder near you who is flooding the marketplace and driving prices down. Pedigree, of course, is also a factor because dogs with papers will certainly bring higher prices than dogs without.

Generally speaking, the more expensive the dog, the better the care it will receive. I suspect that this is true because of more discriminating buyers. That doesn't mean that the free pooch from the Animal League is likely to be mistreated. Rather, it simply suggests that folks often pay better attention to sizeable investments. Personally, I treat my two free dogs exactly the same as my top pedigrees. The unfortunate truth, however, is that dog pounds exist because many folks do otherwise.

Puppy prices can also vary within the litter itself. For instance, if females are in large demand in your area, males will become cheaper. Also, some litters contain what we call a *Runt*. This is the smallest of the lot and will usually bring less. Sometimes, the price decreases as the litter mates get older. On the other hand, when the breeder begins to train his older puppies, he can, and often will, increase the going rate.

CO-OWNERSHIP:

In some cases, purebred registered dogs are co-owned. As the terms imply, both the buyer and the seller have equal say regarding the breeding, showing and sale of a dog. Think of it as a business partnership with one asset—the dog itself. This type of arrangement works well if the parties involved get along well, but if not; it can result in partnership from hell. Unfortunately, most show dogs are co-owned or contracted in some form or another. Since these things often get fairly bloody in the long term, you should avoid any form of co-ownership, unless you are the best of friends. It would also be wise to carefully document the terms of the partnership, including the conditions under which it can be dissolved.

The Lease:

There is an equally awkward joint ownership arrangement called a Lease. I call it, *the long arm of the breeder.* Under this plan, the breeder is reluctant to transfer full or partial ownership of the puppy until certain conditions are agreed to and met. Failure of the buyer to comply will result in the return of the dog to the breeder. Sometimes this can be avoided with a large, pre-agreed settlement upon closing.

Most leases exist under a co-ownership agreement. Here's how it usually works: The breeder sells a dog or dogs to you in return for the first pick of the first two subsequent breedings. In addition, he has exclusive rights to pick the stud and show the dog that he sold to you. You, in turn, get the right to have the dogs live with you, during which time you may train them and assume financial responsibility for any litters that are produced. At such time, as all of the elements of the lease are satisfied, you become the sole owner of the dog. The obvious problem here is that although you are the caretaker of the dog, they are still owned by the breeder; the lease merely designates you as the custodian. Good dogs get titled and poor dogs get fixed, and you get the bill.

This sort of arrangement is much less subjective than co-ownership and does have a clearly defined time limit, however, I would caution the buyer to beware. There are some shady breeders out there offering some equally shady contracts to the unwary soul. Know what you are signing.

Breeding Dogs:

Time to review a few definitions that are important to the discussion of dogs and breeding. As a breeder, I define a *breedable dog* as a bitch that has gone into season, or a stud that has all of his reproductive organs functioning and swimming. The fact that the stud has sired and the bitch has produced live pups makes them both *proven dogs.* An *older dog* is one whose breeding life is nearing an end and will be put out to pasture. Lastly, there is the *breeding dog*, which is one that is currently active in your breeding program. Those dogs that we are not sure of are simply called *adults* or *pups.* The age from which breeding dogs become older dogs will vary according to the sex of the dog. In the case of bitches, the three most likely years are seven, eight, and nine. The point which you decide your dog is ready for the golden age depends on the health of the dog and your personal agenda. For me, nine is pushing it. Studs, however, can generally be used for a longer period of time, providing all the parts are working. If you are going to get a dog specifically for breeding, purchase one between eight months and three years. Avoid four and five-year-old bitches as well as nine-year-old studs unless they are of exceptional quality. Even exceptional lines have greater potential for problems at an older age. Bitches often have tougher times whelping and produce fewer eggs as they age. Studs, on the other hand, can be used past ten or eleven years of age, but they will likely incur many maintenance problems. Before breeding, I advise you to research what you are getting into, start fresh and discard the unimportant stuff. The age of the dog *does* matter because we simply do not know if the adult is even breedable.

For some folks, raising a puppy is the hard part of dog ownership. In purchasing an adult dog, you may be trading one set of tribulations for another. If you purchase an adult dog for the purpose of breeding, be ready for an animal with established habits as well as historical baggage. Allowing for this, you have many preferable options available when purchasing a breeding dog.

As often happens in our modern, mobile economy, many folks are forced to move rather suddenly and must find a new and suitable home for their dog. This is why, the walls of pet supply stores and veterinary offices are filled with advertisements for adult dogs that are available. Remember those breeders who agreed to take back an unsatisfactory puppy sale? Well, they will also be out in the marketplace trying to find a suitable home for a dog that is now an adult.

MIXED BREED VS. PUREBRED:

There is nothing in the archives of wisdom that says mixed breeds cannot be excellent dogs. One of the uncertainties of purchasing a mixed breed, however, is that you will probably not know what the puppy will look like when he grows up. Of course there are also some crossbreeds that are rather dense but the same is also true for purebreds. As far as breeding a mixed breed goes, the only thing I can say is that "accidents can happen fast." Some bad ties do happen and unless somebody opened the gate to let the two out, the blame rests squarely on your shoulders, so, you have three options when this happens.

1– Call the vet immediately if it is an unwanted tie. There is a pill and/ or shot that can be administered (if caught in time) to prevent or abort the pregnancy. It should be administered within forty-eight hours. There is, however, a downside to this procedure. It could induce further complications; therefore, have a serious sit down with your vet before exercising this option.

2– Live with the mistake and treat the litter as a professional. Don't blame the puppies for being born; blame the breeder for not being alert to the problem.

3– You just like having litters so the tie really doesn't matter. Responsibility is not an issue with you.

In summary, as far as mixing of the breeds is concerned, I feel that it is the owner's responsibility to control his animal's breeding activities and be ready to live with the results.

Unregistered Purebred:

Let us now consider the lowest form of dog royalty—the unregistered purebred. There is absolutely nothing wrong with such a dog except there are no papers available to trace his lineage. I know a fellow who has some of the best hunting dogs that I have ever seen and they are all unregistered purebreds with no papers, yet they are all clinically purebred.

Oddly enough, some breeders will sell you a dog without papers, and then charge you an extra fee if you want papers. This makes no sense to me. The price of the dog should always include the cost of pedigree verification. In any case, if you want a dog without papers (unregistered purebred) then inform the breeder and the price might be reduced.

For purposes of breeding, some breeders might be nervous about selling a dog too close to his or her own market. This should never be a problem. If a breeder wishes to restrict the puppies breeding rights, then all he needs to do is to check the restriction box on the papers.

Limited Registration:

Limited registration is designed to limit the breeding rights of the dog's owner. The breeder can only give limited registration to the new owner.

This doesn't restrict the dog from being bred. This simply limits the dog from receiving registration papers from any litter that it produces.

Limited registration prevents dogs from entering and receiving titles in the show world but, does not prevent canines from entering and receiving titles from field trials, hunt tests, and most agility events. The breeder can reverse limited registrations to the owner only if the breeder consents but be weary, the breeder might want something in return, and it will most likely cost the unwary owner. Limited registrations are usually enforced for any of three reasons.

1– The dog may be faulted and the breeder is making sure that the pup is not bred to continue these faults.

2– This is the only way some breeders can retain some control over the litter sold. It is usually an alternative to a co-ownership and can be modified when specific obligations are met within the terms of sale. Most will convert the contract into a co-ownership. See to it that the contract will avoid the conversion of a co-ownership.

3– The breeder is reluctant to have any pups bred, with papers, other than the ones he owns.

CHOOSING A VETERINARIAN:

Unless you already have one from a previous pet, choosing a vet could take a little time. I have two of them-for two very good reasons! One of my veterinarians actually makes house calls. He is very helpful for nails, tail, and shots. In addition, he has lots of constructive ideas regarding raising and caring for my dogs. He is a personable fellow who often takes the time over a cup of coffee to discuss an issue. He also has a low overhead. The second veterinarian is used for surgical procedures, heart worm testing, emergency calls, and more important, this vet has the means to help me with some complicated issues concerning breeding which will be brought up later in this book. Finding a vet who can cover all of the bases is like finding a diamond in the rough. Some vets are more skilled in specific areas than others. In short, I have come to know them both and trust them completely with my dogs.

It can be difficult for the first time dog owner to navigate through the world of veterinary medicine. Some vets will ask if they have treated your dog before, if not, they may tack on a new dog fee along with an emergency visit or examination fee. Be alert to this and ask before making a commitment. I prefer the veterinarian whose home and clinic are on the same property. They may be smaller but they are also more flexible and responsive to emergency situations.

In such cases, your animal will receive prompt, professional medical attention and that is really what it's all about. Understand that there are many fine veterinarians who will move heaven and earth to help your animal, regardless, of where their clinic is located. My observations in this area are fairly general and somewhat subjective. Nevertheless, they have evolved from many years or experience as a breeder and trainer.

BEDDING:

Bedding is a very important aspect to consider. Improper bedding may cost you a perfectly fine breeding animal. Fluffy sleeping quarters that contain certain types of foam might be fine to use as long as it is out of the crate. Inside the crate is another matter, inasmuch as the mattress can easily be torn and consumed due to being bored. The dog can quickly ingest enough foam, which will, in turn, bind his or her intestinal track. Many a fine breeding bitch and stud dogs have been lost because of ingestion of such contaminants.

Ironically, puppies really don't care if they live in the finest house, ride in the finest car, or sleep in an imported bed. They understand sleeping on top of one another in a wooden box that is soft, cozy, warm and quiet. A bunch of old blankets or clothes with no buttons will do just fine for now but when you eventually purchase his permanent bedding, all foam products should be kept out of the crate.

This is Angus. Fast asleep on his mothers legs.
Photo by Tom Dwyer

Thor using the arm rest of a director's chair.
Photo by Tal Alan

My children created a human bed for this GSP pup.
Photo by Tom Dwyer

Nicki, a West Highland White Terrier pup, sleeping solemnly.
Photo by Michele McKechnie.

"Three little scamps"
These pups played for hours around this lawn chair.
Finally, they decided to call it a morning.

Photo by Jane Dwyer

Puppies understand sleeping on top of one another in a
wooden box that is soft, cozy, warm and quiet.

Photo by Tom Dwyer

Cedarbay's Mousse-Man Cometh.
Photo By Marianne Rousseau.

Birdlands Rudy of the Valley with his mother
HMK's Dandy Delts' Surprise.

Photo by Pat Russell

2

Genetics

On the surface, it would seem that when champion dogs are mated, they will regularly produce champion offspring. Unfortunately, this is not always the case. I know of champion sires that were mated with champion bitches and produced litters that had a few nice pups, but the majority of the dogs were mediocre at best. I have also known of champion sires who were mated with non-champion bitches and produced exactly the same mix of pups.

It is important observations for us to consider when we deal with more and more stud owners who are focusing on the appearance of their champion studs. Their primary concern is to create and maintain a *working pedigree* wherein all canines within that pedigree, are *100 percent titled* and *clean* dogs (non-titled dogs) are never used in such breeding programs. Paying too much attention to the dog's purity within the pedigree, instead of the dog's intelligence could lead to thin quality lines. Sacrificing the innate quality of the animal in order to win technical points might make the dog look great but his hereditary instincts will likely become diluted. Ironically, this practice also has the effect of filtering out many of the attributes that made the dog a champion in the first place.

Think of it as a beauty pageant with the swimsuit competition as the only event. This obsession to fix one problem usually leads to the introduction of several other problems depending upon the specific genetic changes being manipulated within the line. Put another way, the selective stud owner is almost always looking to *repair* a perceived problem in his line. This is contrary to the efforts of most other owners who are simply trying to *continue* the basic attributes of an already existing breed. A selective mating for a cosmetic effect accomplishes nothing unless the dog has basic latent intelligence. Breeding dogs must be intelligent and intelligent dogs are the most likely to pass along the best characteristics of the breed. Ask the breeder who has produced the most champions to explain his mate selection strategy, and you will probably discover that his kennels are full of exceptionally bright dogs that includes clean lines. It is a side effect of this beauty vs. brains dilemma that many dog owners who choose not to enter competitions, may very well have the better dog.

COMPLEMENTING:

At a minimum, when you consider breeding your dog, you first make certain that the prospective mate meets the minimum standards for satisfying the accepted properties of the breed. If you are lucky enough, you may even find a mate who shows the potential to actually better the breed. In either case, you are doing what is known as "complementing the breed" or bringing it to perfection.

It has been my experience that this is best accomplished by finding a stud who complements the bitch rather than the other way around. Many times, I have seen many stud owners turn away a perfectly good female on the grounds that she didn't appear "just right." Ironically, I find that the successful litter is more likely to evolve when the owner of the bitch is the one who is more selective.

Once the owner is satisfied that his bitch conforms to the standards of the breed, he should then search for a stud that will improve her line. This is particularly true if the female has a faulty personality or needs some cosmetic improvement. The owner should also try to select a stud that closely resembles his dog, thereby insuring the best complement. Of course, the stud should be of high quality and both dogs should be intelligent. Not everyone can own the very best, but as long as you focus on the highest affordable quality, you'll do just fine. By concentrating on the genes that you want reflected in the litter, you will also be able to explore a greater variety of mating options. For example, why breed to one particular stud when you can breed to the stud's father? Research the pedigree of each prospective mate, and you will know his or her complete mating history. Knowing the dog is everything.

German Shorthaired Pointers Blaze and Roxie.
Photo by
Dave Hebert

It has been my experience to find a stud who complements
the bitch rather than the other way around.

INBREEDING:

Inbreeding occurs whenever two closely related dogs are mated: such as a father to a daughter or a son to a mother. Mating cousins is also considered inbreeding. Owners inbreed their animals primarily to prevent undesirable traits from creeping into their line. This practice almost always causes the negative characteristics of the line to become exaggerated in the resulting litters. Since these undesirable traits are no longer hidden, the breeder will then select only the puppies in the litter who do not have them for use in future breeding. Inbreeding also results in fewer undesirables traits in future litters. It will also bring smaller litters.

Inbreeding also permits infertility to creep into the family line as well as an increase in the occurrence of cleft palate. For better or for worse, all of the family members will also look alike. That figures—they all have the same genes.

LINE BREEDING:

Line breeding occurs when you mate distant relatives to one another. This covers the range from second cousins to great grandparents. This is one of the more popular ways to fine tune a family line. The breeder now has the best of both worlds: common traits without the undesirable side effects.

OUTBREEDING:

Outbreeding means finding a suitable but unrelated mate for your dog. This practice is also known as *out-crossing* your dog. When doing this, one should look for a perfect stud or bitch who promises to complement their existing line. It also happens when the breeder wants to introduce new blood into the line. As popular as line breeding may be, it is always wise to selectively outbreed once and awhile.

CROSSBREEDING:

Crossbreeding happens when you mate two dogs that aren't even the same breed. When this is done arbitrarily, you simply get a litter of mongrels. When it is done selectively, it can result in the beginning of a new and functional breed. Many of today's champion breeds were developed in precisely this way. Breeds, which were cross-complementary, were mated and their puppies were then inbred and crossed again. In breeding circles, this is known as infusing a breed. It is also a polite way of saying that your dual champion Setter was likely descended from a long line of mutts.

DNA TESTING:

There are two general categories of DNA testing. One identifies genetic faults. Some of more popular testing within this category are for, copper, Von Willebrand's Disease, retinal problems and night blindness.

The other category of genetic testing is also valuable because it provides a certified genetic fingerprint of your dog. Simply put, the best way to know without question, that the dog you purchased actually came from the sir and dam listed on your pedigree is through certifiable genetic testing.

Testing for genetic faults is done by The Orthopedic Foundation for Animals, while testing for identification is performed by the American Kennel Club. Neither test is mandatory when breeding registered dogs for the first time; however, I must point out that if you are going to use your stud three times in one year or seven times during the course of the dog's life, then the AKC will require that dog be genetically identified by way of a DNA test. Bitches are exempted from this requirement.

DNA SAMPLES:

Collecting a DNA sample only takes a couple seconds. You merely swipe a saliva swab along the dog's gums and send it a laboratory to be identified and posted. This is a simple and inexpensive procedure and is not required if you are only going to use your male for one or two matings. As noted earlier however, it *is* mandatory if you are going to put your dog on the market to breed more than a couple times.

I like the use of a DNA sample. There is no permanent marking and no metal identification chip inserted in his neck and by any standard, it unequivocally confirms that my dog was the true sire.

O.F.A. & PENNHIP:

It is standard breeding procedure to have your dog's hips checked for dysplasia. There are two ways to go about this: either by the Orthopedic Foundation for Animals, or by using another method called PENNHIP. Although common practice, either tests is not mandatory in order to obtain registered papers for your pup.

In the case of O.F.A.exam, an X-ray of the dog is taken while the animal is placed so that his hip sockets are as perfectly aligned as possible. The X-ray is then examined by three separate and independent veterinarians. Each will rate the hip placement along a graded scale from poor to excellent. You will then receive a graded hip certificate containing the average of their collective judgment.

There are two widely held misconceptions about the OFA certificate regarding its relation to the registration of the dog's pedigree, I must caution you about. I call them "bad doggie rumors."

A.) You must have an OFA certificate which clears your breeding dog or dogs of hip disorders in order for your litter to have a valid registration.

B.) Your dog has to be identified with a tattoo, microchip, and/or DNA sample in order to have a valid OFA certificate.

These misconceptions are so widely held that some veterinary offices often add fuel to the fire by attesting that these "bad doggie rumors" are, in fact, valid certification requirements. Nothing could be farther from the truth. The OFA hip certificate is confirmation of the condition of your dog's hips and that is the extent of it! The AKC and OFA certifications serve two separate needs. You may still breed your dog with both certificates, or you may breed your registered pedigree without his hips being evaluated. It is that simple. The same goes for microchips, tattoos, and DNA samples. They are nice to have; however, they are simply not required in order to get the animal's hips evaluated. Neither are they required for your litter to be registered in kennel clubs. They will result in the placement of the evaluation results in the stud books in the event there is an identifiable genetic or electronic mark, otherwise, the results are merely left out. Either way, your dog's certification is perfectly valid.

If your vet insists on a chip or tattoo, then he is probably has a cash flow problem. The OFA reading on hips is only a check point for breeding a better dog—nothing more.

Moving on, if it is a bitch that you are having evaluated by the OFA, it is best to wait until she is well out of season before having the test done. This could mean the difference between a fair evaluation and a good one. Those who neglect to do this may fail, and wind up having to contact the O.F.A. and explain the circumstances in order to have a retest performed. Chances are that they will be allowed to have the testing redone.

Many folks are concerned with the subjectivity of judgment calls, even if they are being made by trained professionals. If you fall into that group, there is a much more quantitative method available called PENNHIP. During this test (developed at Penn State) the dog is inoculated and placed on a special padded platform where his hips are then displaced. Three

X-rays are then taken and each is then evaluated along a graded numeric scale. For example, after extensive data collection, the typical German Shorthaired Pointer has been found to have an acceptable displacement range from .2 to .3 measured units. In this case, lower is better so, any Shorthair who measures below .2 would be rated excellent while those falling in-between .2 and .3 would be rated average. Any falling between .4 and .5 would be considered fair and those coming in above .5 would be classified as poor or dysplastic. Of course, the acceptable baseline range for a Shorthair will be different than those for other breeds.

Although this is a much more objective standard, I recommend that you supplement such testing with an O.F.A, regardless of its subjectivity—particularly if the Pennhip was done at an early age or the dog belongs to a breed that is prone to dysplasia.

ELBOWS:

The elbows of your breeding dogs are just as important as their hips; however, there does not appear to be as much emphasis on checking for genetically problematic elbows as with hips. Methods of checking for elbow dysplasia have been around for a while however, and its importance is dictated by need, type of dog, and breeders' preference. In addition, some of the problems with inherited genetic diseases of the elbow will present themselves in young dogs as injuries, long before the dog is two—the age when OFA certification is required. One of many diseases that may contribute to elbow and hip problems is Osteochondritis, commonly known as OCD.

If your breeding stock has a history of joint problems, or you are introducing another line with such a history, I would recommend getting the elbows and hips checked in order rule out the possibility of perpetuating these traits. Remember, however, that just because the dogs you are breeding do not seem to posses genetic faults, his or her litter mates might. Therefore, two dogs certifies with excellent hips are still capable of producing a fair hipped dog. Certification will only tell you that there probability of this happening.

It is also good to be wary of diagnostic overkill. Just because your dog is limping doesn't mean that he has a genetic defect. Avoid rushing to judgment because the limp could be nothing more than an injury from roughhouse play. It all comes down to common sense. I personally know of a couple who had their animal receive four separate diagnoses running the gamut from a broken toe to OCD. When they finally took the dog to an experienced vet, they discovered that there was absolutely nothing wrong with the animal. Things that I *would* consider as red flags, however, would be changes in the dog's gait or trot. Look for the paws which turn inward. This places less pressure on the inside of the elbow joint. Also, look for the elbow to have a limited range of motion.

EYES:

The eyes are another part of the dogs anatomy, where undesirable genetic faults will present themselves. Some breeders proudly display certificates declaring that their potential mate is free of any eye abnormalities. The Canine Eye Registration Foundation, (C.E.R.F.) issues such certificates. Retinal Dysplasia, Cataracts, and Eyelid Disorders are just some of the diagnostic categories covered by screening.

Like the OFA testing, tattooing or identifying your dog by use of a microchip is not necessary in order to receive a CERF certification. The Canine Eye Registration Foundation will refuse no dog who applies. A simple "N" is placed next to the certification number if your dog is not identified, however, a non identified canine will not be registered in C.E.R.F.'s database. In any event, you have the certificate in hand.

OSTEOCHONDRITIS DESSICANS:

One of the major causes of elbow dysplasia in large breed dogs can be directly traced to a joint decease called Osteochondritis Dessicans (commonly known as OCD). This condition normally occurs during the early stages of the dog's life where development and growth are increasing at a fast pace. OCD can also result from excessive weight gain. A very high calorie diet containing excessive amounts of calcium also aggravates the problem.

Genetic mismatching of parents can also set the stage for OCD by causing the lack of calcification within the cartilage which will eventually thicken, degenerate, and die. The end product is an adult dog with cracked and weakened cartilage that is not fully attached to the bone.

It is also important to understand that OCD will affect the entire body, not just merely one joint or one bone. Conversely, inflammations, fractures, infections, and play related injuries, could well be the problem rather than OCD. A rush to judgment would be premature.

I suggest letting a competent veterinarian call the shots when treating your dog's problem as an injury. For your part, restrict your dog's physical activity by limiting any excessive shoulder or elbow movement. Then, when the dog gets older, have elbow x-rays taken and submit them to the Orthopedic Foundation for Animals for elbow certification.

CANCER:

Cancer has evolved as one of the main killers in older canines. Most owners are just beginning to recognize precisely how rapidly the incidence of cancer has grown. The larger problem is why?

Cancer has likely been around dogs just as long as it has with humans. For some reason, however, we have failed as pet owners in the area of cancer prevention. I have always felt that the many forms of chemicals and toxins (either dietary or airborne) which we expose our dogs to, result in a greater chance for certain types of cancer to develop. It has also been suggested that cancer may be linked to a genetic predisposition, but I am still waiting for solid research that will weigh in on that argument.

We are responsible for the lifelong care of our pets. It follows then that we should, be extremely wary of *chemicals and toxins*. What is a carcinogen for man is probably not good for the canine either. Add this to the fact that dogs cannot communicate as effectively as we do when we are ailing. We, the pet owners, must be alert enough to keep them out of harms way. The problem may not surface in the dog's younger years, but you will certainly see it when the dog gets older.

Some canines are bred while owners are unaware that either mate may have some form of cancer. Tumors are discovered in some bitches shortly after mating. Some studs are also found to have cancer at a very young age and despite treatment, continue to sire as many pups as they can—all the while freezing semen for future insemination. Breeding two dogs with a history of cancer at such an early age is a red flag issue when it comes to bettering the bred. We need to rethink this entire practice.

CRYPTORCHIDISM:

When dogs, like most other animals are first born, their testicles are usually located somewhere near their kidneys. After a short time, they usually migrate down a canal into the scrotum. Sometimes the dog may be lacking the male hormone testosterone thereby preventing the downward movement of the testicles. Things become further complicated by the natural closure of the canal after a period of about five months. If they have not moved by then, the trapped testicles will eventually develop tumors and will have to be surgically removed. This could happen in nine months or in nine years.

I have been advised that those dogs who are so affected, are perfectly breedable males, however, there is a general reluctance to use them for fear of a recurrence in any of the litters they may produce.

As far as the medical community is concerned, there is a definite consensus that this phenomenon, called Cryptorchidism, is a genetic defect. I have contacted both genetic and veterinary university departments and been told that it was clearly a predisposition toward a genetic disorder. However when I asked to be directed to qualified research studies in this area, they were unable to point to any. One geneticist told me with certainty that this was a genetic trait while admitting that he couldn't refer me to any supportive data. There has been much research done that categorizes bilateral, unilateral, and partial retention, as well as delayed migration of the testicles and although I agree that this is likely a genetic disorder, I am yet to find any hard evidence supporting this conclusion.

Muscle tension within the stomach and legs will indeed
raise the testicles back up into their respected canals.
Relaxing these same muscles will slowly send the
testicles back into their individual sacks.
Many such repetitions could prevent one or more testicles from
descending. Such an injury could make the retention permanent.

**Tom Dwyer along with Fred Newcomb and Dancer.
Photo By Pat Russell**

When it comes to breeding a dog with unilateral retention, (one
testicle) I would be concerned about the retained testicle's ability to
become malignant rather than its inconclusive genetic potential. I know
of many unilateral animals that are currently active in the breeding circuit.
One, whose owner makes no secret of it, is highly regarded as breeding

stock, and whose pups are sired having two testicles. Another aspect of this problem is the widespread use of the bitches whose litter mate brothers are defined as cryptorchids while the owners know full well that the gene has an equal opportunity to reappear in the bitches as well as their siblings. The same risk is evident with male litter mates who do not currently have the problem although their brothers do. The term "snip-em if you do not see-em and breed-en if you do" (however primitive) is currently practiced, but may not be the best medicine until the jury is in on this subject.

MANGE:

Mites cause Demodex, Cheyletiella, or Scrcoptic mange, and bear in mind that almost every dog has mites. It follows that any increase in the mite population on the dog, will, in effect, increase the likelihood of mange growing proportionately. The dog's immune system generally keeps these mites in check and conversely, any increase in the mite's population can thus be linked to a weakened immune system. Simply put, the mite's population increases when the dog's immune system weakens. It has been argued that the strength of the immune system is a genetic trait; however, I am yet to be convinced that there is a gene/mite causal relationship.

It is known that dog's have a greater chance of contracting mange during different stages of their life cycle, andas I have noted, most dogs usually fight off the spread of mite infestation for their entire lives. Many articles have been written about mange and the mite, along with proper diagnosis and treatment which include many contradictory articles that advocate neutering and spaying as a solution. In truth, neutering your dog will not get rid of mange, nor will it prevent it from happening. The proper course of action is to find out why your dog contracted mange in the first place. The immune system works less efficiently during the early stages of puppyhood, in sick canines, and in very old dogs. Other factors which reduce the animal's ability to fight off mites are puberty, certain foods, electronic fencing and chemicals.

Let's start with puberty. Most breeders will not breed their dogs until at they are at least two years of age, but dogs really don't care about time lines and are not always inclined to wait for their reproductive organs to mature. The fact is, a male canine can breed at the ripe young age of eight months, which is coincidental with the occurrence of a bitch in her first heat. Hormonal changes usually start and end at around that age. This gives the mite a large window of opportunity.

Food should be your next concern. A good strong food base has always been the basic foundation for maintaining a dog's coat which is why food manufacturers are prone to sing praises about their additives. At this moment, I am looking at a bag of dog food which I use regularly. The front and back of the package state that it contains three omega fatty acids which are great for your dog's coat and aids in the regulation of his immune system. Unfortunately, however, we too often cave in to supermarket sales and coupon specials which result in the compromise of dog food quality. The resultant economic juggling of foods can compound your dog's dietary deficiencies and bring about intestinal irregularity as well as a weak dull coat—increasing the odds in favor of the mite.

Electronic fencing is the new cure-all for wandering pets. Let's say that the house next to you was just sold to a new neighbor that thinks his land extends to Mars and all the birds flying over his property also belong to him. It follows that any other creature including your dog must fall into the same category. In this situation, electronic fencing can prove to be invaluable. It is an extremely efficient method of keeping your dog home without the use of a chain. Unfortunately, many dogs are being introduced to the fence at too early an age and at too high an electrical charge. Stress, in this form, leads to an increase of mange in very young dogs. Electronic fences are beginning to take the place of basic family training. This is an unfortunate phenomenon but it has surfaced none the less.

Finally, we come to the introduction of chemicals. The list of things that our animals absorb and ingest is long indeed: lawn fertilizers, dips, new and experimental vaccinations, ingestible flea pills, once a month wormers and heart worm pills (considered toxins), plant consumption (both the garden and the household varieties), floor cleaners, and shampoos. Obviously, we would never swallow this stuff ourselves; nonetheless, we unconsciously expose our animals to chemicals such as these on a regular basis. The problem is complicated because when our dogs ingest those chemicals, the symptoms of mange become camouflaged. In our rush to judgment, we think what we see is mange but, in reality, we are seeing the animals' reaction to the Sodium Bisulfate in the cleaner that we spilled on the floor. Although it has been suggested that genetic traits may be one of the reasons for a weakened immune system, it is entirely possible that you and I contribute equally to the problem.

Mange has also been misdiagnosed as a flea allergy or other sensitive skin conditions so, get the facts before rushing into surgery. Any genuine genetic immune system deficiency will appear repeatedly and result in the dog undergoing a very long recovery period. So, do not fix your dog for mange, fix his defective immune system.

**Millbrook's Miss Elle as a pup.
Photo by Jane Dwyer**

**Miss Elle, at two years of age, with owner Tracy Banfield.
Photo by
Dave Banfield**

3

Non-Genetics

Since the dawn of civilization, the dog breeding world has focused on the elimination of undesirable genetic characteristics. Most of the headaches associated with this effort have evolved from the assumption that problem genes are best eliminated through the process of selected inbreeding. This occurs when animals are mated within their immediate families. As noted in chapter 2, this practice may also include a line breed member of the extended family such as a second cousin. The inherent problem is that selected breeding concentrates so much on breeding for pedigree *per se*, it often ignores the dog's health which is certainly as important as the breeding process itself. Unfortunately, this oversight has resulted in many a mated bitch fighting for her life against viruses, parasites, vaccinations, and certain supplements which they should not be exposed to while gestating a litter of pups.

Having said all that, let's take a look at some of the more common problems that owners and breeders should to be concerned about.

BLOOD WORK:

A simple blood test is the best way to determine if your bitch is likely to have any non-genetic whelping complications when breeding. Chemical analysis, along with a complete blood count will determine if all her organs and glands are working well. I also look for vitamin and mineral balances, especially in older bitches. A slight imbalance or total deficiency in this area could mean something else is wrong with the bitch and subsequently, should influence your decision to mate. One example of such a deficiency would be with the calcium levels. Low levels of calcium affect gestation and have been linked to seizures.

A word of caution, however, blood work will not forecast the genetic predisposition of the pups. The focus of the CBC is on the health of the bitch and her ability to whelp a healthy litter. This is especially important when dealing with older bitches. Blood work is one of those extra things you could have done in order to effectively monitor the health of your mature dogs. On the other hand, blood work is not really necessary for younger animals. I choose have a set of diagnostics done when the dog is about two years of age. These reports can then be used for comparison as the dog ages. For example, you could combine a CBC test with yearly blood work testing such as Brucellosis, heart worm. The same type of blood work can be performed again when the animal is as old as eight. You can now compare both results and look for trends in your animal's condition. Such as how well the Thyroid is working in your older bitch. This is important because Thyroid levels can be linked to autoimmune problems.

HEART MURMUR:

A heart murmur is a leaky valve and, as in any plumbing system, leaky valves can occur for many reasons. Some of the major culprits are fevers, anemia, whelping, aging, stress and the wear and tear on the heart muscles. I would argue, however, that the jury is still out when relating these murmurs to genetic traits.

I personally try to avoid breeding a bitch who has been diagnosed with a leaky valve because of the stress that is involved in the whelping process itself. When a bitch develops a valve problem after whelping, however, it will have no bearing on the medical condition of the pups. I would; nevertheless not use that bitch again until the valve has healed, inasmuch as the same problem is certain to recur. Sires who stud with the same problem can continue to stud; nevertheless, good breeding etiquette dictates that this or any other medical diagnoses be disclosed. Furthermore, if any pups are born with a heart murmur, the problem must also be disclosed to potential buyers; inasmuch as a great deal of time will be required to monitor these pups to adulthood. Fortunately most puppy murmurs are fairly mild.

If by chance, a breeder consistently sees a moderate but steady amount of leaky valves from a succession of litters, then the bells should be sounding a warning to definitely change either the way they are bred, or the dogs themselves.

GIARDIASIS:

Giardiasis is the infection of the small intestine caused by the parasitic protozoan **Giardia Lamblia.** The disease is contracted most commonly through poor personal hygiene, contact with an infected animal, or sexual contact. It may also results from drinking untreated water or eating contaminated food. Symptoms of Giardiasis may also include mild to severe diarrhea, nausea, abdominal cramps, poor appetite, and fatigue.

This means double trouble because Giardiasis is readily transmitted to humans. How often have you seen your dogs lick the face of your children and their playmates? How many times you have unwittingly drank from the same container that your dog might have licked. It's scary but it is a very real danger. This is another one of those cases where treating the symptoms is your dogs best bet. Preventing the ailment beats curing it any day.

BRUCELLOSIS:

Brucellosis presents itself in many forms: undulant fever, which is an extension of the word *undulating; i.e.,* up-and-down fever, Bangs' disease, with its contagious abortions, Malta fever, named for the place of it's origin on the island of Malta, Goat fever which is found in goat milk, and finally, in Mediterranean and Rock fevers. Whatever form it takes, Brucellosis was named after it's discover, the British physician, Sir David Bruce, who first identified it in 1887. The bacterium is considered rare in the United States but when it does surface here, it is as a predominantly bovine disease generally occurring in the herds of bison, reindeer, goats, hogs and cattle of the western states. Fortunately for humans, the problem is controlled through the pasteurization of milk and the use of a cattle vaccination named Strain 19. Brucellosis usually spreads by way of contaminated discharge, vaginal expulsion, including aborted fetuses, and placenta. Unfortunately for canines, there is no known cure to date for Brucellosis, and although the symptoms disappear, the underlying bacteria still remains present. Dogs contaminated in this fashion sometimes unwittingly come into contact with other dogs, so, there is ample reason to view contamination as a serious problem among breeding bitches and well traveled stud dogs.

Mating with an infected bitch would, in essence, end the career of your stud dog because any further mating on his part would only compound the contamination problem. Although there is an effective treatment in place, proper diagnosis and treatment of this disease will most likely leave you with a sterile stud. Accordingly, untreated bitches will usually abort their litters. In any event, the whole mess is the result of sloppy, unprofessional breeding.

If the person whose dog you are breeding with asks for a negative Brucellosis test as a breeding prerequisite, then by all means, accommodate him. You have probably spent more money having the animal's hips examined for dysplasia, heart murmurs, and testing for genetic faults which present themselves in the eyes. If on the other hand, you feel that the Brucellosis test is too much trouble, then try and find another breeder who feels the same way, but be advised, you may be unable to find anyone who will accept your terms.

CHOCOLATE:

Over the years, many folks have told me that their dogs can eat chocolate without complications. These owners undoubtedly have never heard of theobromine which is related to caffeine and promotes seizures in canines. It can also affect the heart, kidneys, and central nervous system. Although different dogs react differently to theobromine, it is not good for any of them and even though the animal doesn't show an immediate reaction, it doesn't mean that you should allow him to continue eating chocolate. I would also make sure he avoids coffee, landscaping chips containing cocoa, along with over fifty additional plants containing theobromine.

WORMS:

All worms are dangerous to your dog but heartworm is far and away the worst. The best way to combat this parasite is to have the dog tested once a year during his annual examination and supplement this with periodic worming medications.

Most dogs infected by the heartworm will tire quickly and, in more advanced cases, collapse entirely. Sometimes, they will also have a slight hacking cough. Any or all of these symptoms should send you off to the vet as soon as possible. As in the case of humans, never attempt to shortcut the problem by using medicine that was prescribed for another dog. Most medications are to *prevent* the heartworm in it's early stages of life but will do little, if anything, for the animal who is already infected by an egg-laying adult worm. Monthly heartworm treatments will not kill the adult worm because they are specifically designed to eliminate these parasites before they reach adulthood.

Currently, there are two ways for you to prevent heartworm in your animal. The first way is by giving your dog a regular monthly pill—the second way is by giving him a yearly shot. Both methods will work: nevertheless, the methodology you choose will be dictated by two considerations.

1. If your dog has a negative reaction to the shot, there is no recourse; whereas, with the pill, you can stop at any given point during that particular treatment and change medications.
2. Age can also be a factor. Many breeders feel that the organs of older dogs have a harder time with stronger-based medications. It might be prudent, therefore, to use the yearly shot on young healthy dogs while using the monthly pills on pups and older animals.

Hookworms, whipworms, and roundworms, although not as serious a problem, can effectively be controlled by taking preventive measures. Bringing a recent stool sample to the vet during the animal's annual checkup is always advisable. If you don't worm your dog periodically, then there is a good chance that he or she will eventually become infected by some kind of worm. A good indicator that your dog might have a major infection would be a noticeable amount of runny stools, combined with a ginger walking gate. Given these, you might well have a serious problem.

Most breeders like to have their dogs well wormed before breeding. Worming the dog once a year or just when your dog is about to go into season will not fix the problem if your dog is already infected. Worms, especially round worms, will show up a few weeks after the whelping period. A monthly or a periodic worming well before mating will give you better piece of mind.

Some breeders in the northern sections of the country often choose to eliminate the heartworm medication in a breeding bitch during the winter months because, during that time, there are no mosquitoes to infest the bitch or her pups. They will then have the bitch retested, after weaning. I personally choose not to use any worming agent, heart worm agent, pain killer, vaccination, medications, or vitamin supplements, (unless directed by my veterinarian) from the time the bitch has gone into season, until she is fully weaned from the pups. If any of the above medications were needed, then the bitch should not have been bred in the first place.

HYPERTROPHIC OSTEODYSTROPHY:

Hypertrophic Osteodystrophy (HOD) is a disease that causes a swelling of the joints. It occurs primarily in young, large medium and large breed dogs, and in some cases, can be extremely painful. It has been my experience that this condition is not usually diagnosed until another injury affecting the leg or shoulder surfaces, causing the canine to become lame. Many owners will tend to dismiss such lameness as the result of aggressive play and trust that it will simply go away: consequently, any reliable diagnosis is delayed. There is some speculation that this condition develops after the administration of vaccinations. Another theory holds that there are too many dairy products (such as cottage cheese) included in the dog's diet which deposit more calcium than needed in the growing pup. Personally, I believe that both could be the culprits.

In either event, you must deal with the underlying problem. In order to accomplish this, you should keep your dog's diet as balanced as possible. Supplements may be added for the short term only. Specifically, you must, reduce, monitor, and regulate the calcium intake normally found in your dogs food for the duration of his or her life. The religious use of quality food will take the guesswork out of this a task. Also, try not to over vaccinate your dog. Give him his shots only when needed. New and developing vaccines might also give you new and developing problems.

Second, get a proper diagnosis. Make sure the vet knows all you are doing with the dog and have all vaccination records up to date.

Third, be careful concerning the use of pain killers. For the most part, painkillers are often considered to be a good thing; however, their casual use might cause additional problems. A dog that limps knows he is in pain. If he is in too much pain then he will hold his leg up pick up and consequently slow down his activity. This will show you that something is wrong. Painkillers give a false sense of security to the injured dog. By their nature, they mask the pain and will result in the animal to putting more pressure on his joints than he should. This, of course, will only exacerbate the injury, and will lead to surgery or a long and painful (never mind expensive) recovery. If, on the other hand, you find that painkillers are an absolute necessity, then find a way to humanely restrict the animal's movements during the recovery period.

You should be patient when dealing with Hypertrophic Osteodystrophy. In most cases, the problem can resolve itself. However; left unchecked, HOD could travel into the hips, which further complicates matters. I have used 600 milligrams of glucosamate and vitamin C, but only for short periods. Your dog's condition will last some time, so be sure to check in regularly with your vet.

LYME DISEASE SHOTS:

Lyme disease infects your dog via a tic—most likely a deer tic. Rocky Mountain Spotted Fever Disease is another less common but just as troublesome tic transmitted disease and is transmitted by way of a tic bearing the same name. Although there are many collars and pills available on the market, an immunization shot has surfaced as the method of choice in the prevention from contracting the disease. Keeping tics off in the first place, is best accomplished by using dips, collars and pills. I prefer not give my dogs a lyme shot until a reputable injection is developed because the after effects can be brutal. For example, your dog could actually get the disease from the shot, and small tumors may also develop at the point of injection. Also, I prefer not to use pills or collars. My treatment of choice is to administer a liquid dip behind the animal's shoulder as well as the use of cedar bedding when traveling. I am particularly careful about this practice, except for cedar bedding, when dealing with pregnant bitches and ready to use stud dogs. My personal reasons for carefully monitoring the use of chemicals is that most dips and wormers are also toxins and as I stated earlier in this chapter, one less toxin in a pregnant bitch is one less problem to worry about.

NEUTERING THE DOG:

Sooner or later, this issue crosses the mind of just about every dog owner. Although the questions as to wether or not to neuter a dog is up to you, the question of when to neuter is best taken up with your veterinarian. Personally, I know of three considerations that hold sway in the discussion of whether or not to neuter.

1. Some vets live off the procedure.end of subject.
2. No more puppies.
3. Studies report that neutered dogs bite less. (how much less is the question)

If you're purchasing a puppy with no intent of breeding him, then I would suggest having the dog fixed as soon as possible. Schedule the procedure with your veterinarian. If, on the other hand, you are unsure about the possibility of breeding, then I suggest you delay the decision until the dog reaches the age of two. This should give you enough time to see how the dog develops physically.

Delaying surgery can be an important consideration in the case of females, what with their constant need for clean up of seasons. By the time she is two years old, she will have had four heat cycles and there will be a long line of eligible bachelors wandering around your property—leash laws or not. For the first time owner, who is unsure about breeding, the first heat will likely be enough to send him to the vet.

A male is usually ready to breed at about eight months while the females are ready at their first heat cycle which can occur any time between six months and two years of age. Even then, it is uncertain if she can be mated. So what does one do?

Personally, I would never submit a puppy to surgery before six months of age. Common sense dictates that you wait until he or she is old enough to handle the surgery. Why would you want to do it any earlier?

Blaze and Roxie
Photo by
Dave Hebert

Marianne Rousseau with puppy, Cedarbay's Mousse-Man Cometh.
Photo by
Marianne Rousseau.

A beautiful head shot of Mousse as an adult.
Photo by
Marianne Rousseau.

Blaze and Roxie
Photo by
Dave Hebert

4

Mating

Much of the information available to breeders is general in nature and does not readily lend itself to hands-on problem solving. It is the intent of this chapter, therefore, to focus on the specific actions that owners can and should take so as to breed their dogs in a simple and informed manner. Fortunately, breeding is a natural process and is best handled by the dogs themselves; consequently, the vast number of litters produced are usually problem free. This does not mean that serious problems can't surface during whelping that might jeopardize the well being of your pups, however, most can be smoothed over if we know how to anticipate them. Some of the more important concerns are:

STUD ARRANGEMENTS:

Stud fees differ widely from breeder to breeder. Stud owners may opt for a pre-negotiated dollar fee, the pick of the litter, or both. These fees may, in turn, also depend upon whether or not, you utilize the services of a local dog or send your animal away to be bred. Most breeders know one another personally and consequently require just an oral contract but, unless you have such a relationship, I recommend that you get everything in writing.

In the case of a pick-of-the-litter contract, the stud owner might elect to visit the litter about a week or two after the pups are born for a preliminary inspection. However, the majority of stud owners will elect to visit the litter at approximately six, or even eight weeks after they are born. This time frame corresponds with the pups having been fully weaned, and living on their own. The only difference between six weeks and eight weeks is simple weight gain and personality development of their personalities. Although, the stud owner has eight weeks to pick his dog, six weeks should be adequate. It is important to note that unless it is otherwise stipulated via a formal agreement, in the event that there is only one surviving member of the original litter—it belongs to him. Another problem with this type of arrangement is that if the stud owner is specifically looking for a male or female, the agreement may prevent you from accepting deposits for any of the other litter mates until the stud owner selects his specific dog. If this is going to be a problem, it may be more advantageous for you to simply pay a stud fee and avoid the hassle.

There are also some unwritten niceties you should be aware of before sending your dog out to stud. Some of these simple rules have from time to time, been broken or abused; nevertheless, these rules are the staple of breeding etiquette and should be respected by one and all. If you are using your stud as a service in producing a litter for another breeder for a fee, they are as follows:

1. This fee is either in the form of a pick of one or more pups in the litter or a straightforward monetary fee.
2. Monetary compensation should be paid when service is rendered. Not when *live pups* are produced. If the mating produces still born pups or no pups after a normal whelping period, the stud serviced is not considered a valid mating. In such cases, all fees should be refunded or another mating should be given for free.
3. Stud owners do not own any of the pups in question until the litter owner actually transfers a pup to the stud owner.
4. Pups cannot be registered with papers until the stud owner signs the paperwork as the *certified* stud owner. This type of paperwork should be signed at the time of mating, however, it may also provided by the dam owner shortly after the pups are whelped. This is particularly important in the case where monetary compensation was the method of payment. So, unless both owners have been doing business with each other for years, beware that once the paperwork is out of your hands so; will be your payment leverage. Get paid up front, sign the paperwork, and send it in.
5. One mating producing one pup is a proven breeding. If a pup is payment then the stud owner will own that dog when pup is delivered.

6. Make use of the litter owner and pick up the puppy once it is fully weaned and given its first shots. Let the dam owner raise your pup for the full eight week term.

7. Stay away from all other third parties. Remember the co-ownership and leased dogs I mentioned in the first chapter? They always involve third party coordinators or brokers and they work only for their own interest. The pups that are being produced are for them. The stud and bitch that you own are only hosts. If you own one of these dogs, then you most likely have to work through your broker every time you breed. In any event, as a stud owner, your task is to have your dogs sire pups and to be compensated for it—nothing more.

If you elect to send your bitch away to be mated, be sure to send her as close to her season as possible. Also consider that some states might require quarantine periods for out-of-state animals and your bitch might need time to adjust to her new environment.

SEASON:

The average heat cycle for females is 20 days. This is defined as coming into season. Generally, the temperature in the bitch will rise, giving the rise to the term *going into heat*. The heat cycle or season, will be the only time where the female will accept a male for reproduction.

About a week before the mating cycle begins, the bitch's vulva will swell, her appetite will increase and she may become restless. During the next ten days, there will be a bright red discharge. This discharge will gradually become pink or lighter in color and finally cream-like. During this time, she will also become be more playful with other dogs. She will usually mate with a stud from the tenth to the sixteenth day of her season. Some bitches will even go as far as to mate on the eighteenth day. Although she is still technically in season from the eighteenth day until about the twentieth day, she will probably ugly and growl and snap at her potential suitors.

Odd Seasons:

In the natural course of events, some bitches may have longer seasons than others. These heat cycles might even go on for several months. Although some bitches will only go into heat once a year, others will go into season three or four times a year—the norm being every six months. Separately, they can be handled as normal reproductive cycles for that particular dog; however, the combination of these conditioned in one bitch could be a warning of a serious health problem. Although such abnormalities exist in only a very small percentage of bitches, you as the breeder, should understand that there could be another underlying problem with the dog's reproductive system. Of course, the health of the bitch is your primary concern, so, be certain that there are no internal problems before you consider breeding this particular animal during these times.

Split Season:

Some seasons tend to stop in the middle of their cycles, and for some strange reason, pick up again at some later date. This would be called a *split season* and I always avoid breeding a female during this time.

In the first place, I have no real idea when she is going to finish her cycle. She might not even go into season again until her next scheduled heat which might also be the completion of her first cycle. Many breeders consider this event as an extra heat and assume she is going into season at odd times assuming that the bitch is having an *odd season.*

In the second place, one has no idea if she was receptive during the original season, or if she is going to be receptive when she starts up again; consequently, you could be chasing smoke and unless you and your vet are alert to this problem, you should simply forget the whole thing and wait till she goes into a normal season.

Thirdly, there may have been a physical problem which caused the split season to occur in the first place. This could have been caused by stress, chemical ingestion, or internal reproductive problems. At the risk of belaboring the obvious, breeding your dog should not take precedence over her health and from a purely practical point of view, you will rarely get a successful breeding during a split season.

MATING:

As I mentioned earlier, the best time for mating is usually between the 10th and the 16th day of the heat cycle, although the bitch might be responsive during the 8th & 9th days. One test for receptivity is to scratch the female's hindquarters. If her tail dramatically moves in that direction, she is ready. On the other hand, if her tail stays down, do not mate her. Another reliable barometer of readiness is when she repeatedly sits on her tail when approached by a stud. Basically she is telling him that a longer courtship will be required. The most reliable sign would be tail turning (called flagging) with the playfulness of the bitch (called bucking). Both are positive indicators and should give a breeder cause to start mating.

In any event, by the 16th day, many females start becoming less receptive and the odds for success diminish accordingly. Lastly, a smear test is also available from your veterinarian that will let you know whether or not it is the correct time to mate your dog. This may require several trips to his office but it will greatly improve the likelihood of a successful mating.

Some bitches (particularly younger ones) might have a different breeding time or longer heat cycle. Generally, however, as the dog ages, her season might conform more to the norm of the majority. Therefore, if you have a bitch who generally takes a male on the late end of her heat cycle, (say the 14th to the 16th day) she might, as she ages, start accepting males as early on as the 8th or 10th day. Finally, it is a natural fact of breeding that bitches will start dropping fewer eggs and produce smaller litters as they get older.

The time when your dog goes into a season will also likely vary as you introduce more bitches into your kennel. If for example, your bitches all go into season at different times throughout the year, you will soon find that the first bitch going into a season will tend to (but not always) draw the other bitches into a concurrent season. An example of this phenomenon would be if you have three bitches who go into a season in July, September, and November respectively, you might see them change after a few years to July, August, and late August seasons. Also, remember that female pups who were whelped by one particular female will likely adopt the same season pattern as their mother.

First time mating can be most difficult. Bitches who have been spoiled or pampered by their owners will often tend to fight off any potential suitors. To get around this problem, let the dogs get to know each other in an enclosed area. Who knows what might happen after dinner and a couple of drinks? If on the other hand, the stud is too aggressive, two handlers may be required.

Some first time bitches might even require a muzzle and leash during the mating process. If the experience is that unpleasant for her, then you may want to consider not mating her again. This doesn't mean that she will be a bad mother but rather, she simply doesn't like the mating process itself.

Depending on your stud contract, (assuming you have one) two or three matings may be required before an ample litter size is achieved. This is particularly true when a stud has not been used regularly and is unable to provide sufficient fertilization. When this happens, any stud owner who values his reputation will likely offer his dog's services for free during the next heat cycle.

It would seem appropriate at this time, to become familiar with some mating trade talk. For example, when a stud is trying to mate, he is actually trying to mount the bitch and attempt to make a *connection*. When he successfully connects, then it is called a *tie*. During the tie the male will successfully try to take his hind leg and bring it over so that he is facing south and the bitch is facing north or east west, or southeast, or whatever. They are not facing each other and are joined in an opposite direction.

A bitch that is ready to mate is considered *receptive*. Some mild help is given to the bitch by holding her head, or tucking her head between your legs. Some mild help might be given to the male by slightly lifting the vulva while the male is trying to penetrate.

FIRST ATTEMPT:

If all goes well, the first attempt should be perfectly natural inasmuch as the male and female will play for a short while after which a mounting will ensue and a tie is made. They will stay connected, facing in opposite directions for about fifteen to twenty-five minutes. In the normal course of events they will then pull apart and go about their ways. Life would be grand if it always happened this way but alas, there are a few matings that might require some intervention on your part.

I will call this the *second attempt*. Here are a few tips on what to look for and what to do.

1. The bitch is ready but the stud is not proven and knows not what to do. Go to the *second attempt*.
2. The bitch growls, snaps at the stud 2nd constantly sits on her tail. She might not be receptive yet. Try again in two days. If still unreceptive then try again with *a second attempt*.

Bitches that are in season will be very playful. There will be a lot of nudging or "bucking", in order to gain attention.

Bitches will also be very receptive as the male closely inspects her vaginal area.

Flagging of the tail to one side means that she is ready to be mated.

The stud then mounts the bitch in order to enter or "make a connection".

A successful connection is called a *tie*. During the tie the male will try to take his hind leg and bring it over so that he is facing south and the bitch is facing north or east west, or southeast, or whatever.

They will stay connected, facing in opposite directions for about fifteen to twenty-five minutes. In the normal course of events they will then pull apart and go about their ways.

Here once again is Tom White's stud dog Saddles,
being mated to the bitch, Penny.
We will be following the whelping and rearing of this
breeding throughout the course of this book.

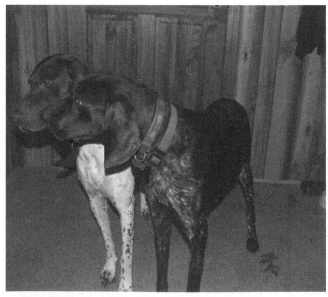

A small adjustment like bringing the dogs into an enclosed
area, will allow the two to concentrate more on each other.
Bucking is more receptive.

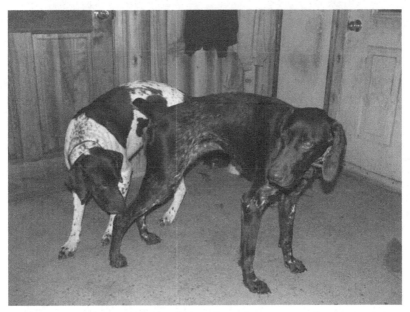

This in turn leads to a better examination.

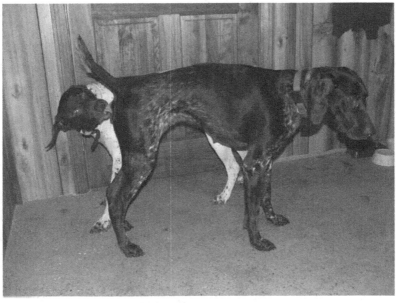

Flagging of the tail.

Stud then mounts and tries to connect and create a tie.

Photos by
Tom Dwyer

SECOND ATTEMPT:

The second attempt should still be natural; however, a little guidance might be required. Place your arm under the hips of the bitch. This will allow the male to investigate closer and will start to clean the bitch. If things move along in their natural order, this is all he will need to attempt a mount. Bear in mind however, that just because he mounts her does not mean he can connect. Even though he has the reflexes, he might not know where to go. His pelvis has to get closer to the rear of the bitch. In the event that you still have one hand under the hips of the bitch, take your left hand, place it under the rump of the male and push it closer until he starts moving faster and faster. Try and raise the vulva to make the procedure easier for the stud. He should soon be connecting. You will have a tie when he stops moving his hips.

You still cannot leave once a connection has been achieved. The dogs still have to turn away (that east/west thing). Also an inexperienced stud might want to pull out which will be more painful for him than it would be for the bitch. You might have to grab both sets of hips and prevent them from separating. At the very least, you should hold onto the collar of the female and wait. This might require that you remain on your knees for the full twenty minutes or so.

What happens when everything works well but you still cannot get a tie because the tail of the bitch is in the way? If that happens, you are going to have to pull it to one side so that the stud can make the connection. The rest is up to him. What's that you say? You already have one arm under the bitch and the other under the studs' rump? This is a rather awkward situation isn't it? At this point, you have three choices. You could let go of the bitch's hips and move her tail or, you could get the assistance from another breeder (who you so wisely had available), or you could proceed to the *third attempt*. Some additional things might still interfere with the successful mating of these two selected animals. The stud could still need some help, or the bitch, although receptive, is still playing hard to get by snapping and sitting.

**A little mating guidance might be required. Place your
arm under the hips of the bitch. This will allow the male
to investigate the bitch with less resistance.**

This is all the stud will need to attempt a mount.

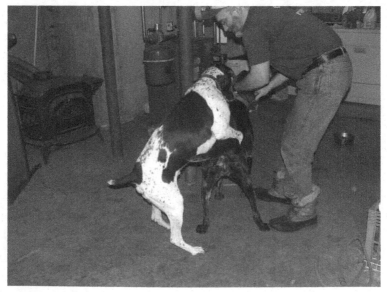

**Bear in mind, just because he mounts the bitch,
doesn't mean he can make a connection.**

Some mild help might need to be given to the male when trying to penetrate. The bitch's tail might also have to be moved.

THIRD ATTEMPT:

Believe it or not, more matings fall into this category than you might imagine. In the case of the growling bitch, mating can be still achieved, however, you will need about six more pairs of hands.

If another breeder can't be found then I would suggest confining or leashing the front of the bitch so that she can't move or turn her head in the direction of her rear. This will free you up to work on the mating end. I recommend at this point, having a beach towel handy. You will thank me later. Place your arm under the bitch as before and use your second hand to either move the tail, or raise the vulva to help the stud. The bitch will still growl but will be unable to react to the mount. Although she will likely calm down after the connection and ensuing tie, be aware, that the bitch may continue to be uncooperative and might still want to sit down for a little revenge. In order to prevent this, place the beach towel under her abdomen, then stand up (inasmuch as kneeling for twenty minutes does nothing for one's back) and use it as a brace preventing her from sitting. The male will stand there and will pull himself free when the time is right. A word of caution about the inexperienced stud—he will want to leave very early. Prevent him from doing so.

There is a slim chance that the bitch might still fight hard during any number of the above attempts. If this occurs, you might wish to use a muzzle if you think it might bring about a successful tie. If by chance you have a bitch who will simply not accept a male, under any condition, then the only other choice for mating would be by artificial insemination.

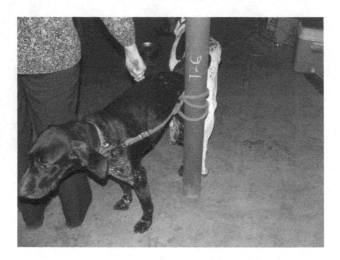

If help can't be found then I would suggest confining or leashing the front of the bitch so that she can't move or turn her head in the direction of her rear. This will free you up to work on the mating end.

Artificial Insemination:

In most cases where the female will have nothing to do with the male, artificial insemination must be used to impregnate her. It is also used when the desired male is geographically too far away to mate. Semen from the stud is shipped frozen and then introduced into the bitch by a qualified technician.

Artificial insemination is starting to become the "breeding method of choice." The down sides are that this method is much more expensive and the litters are smaller; nevertheless, modern technology is beginning to catch up to nature as far as the storage and shipment of sperm, and professional insemination, are a concerned. It is also a very convenient technique when both dogs are living in different parts of the country. No transportation of the bitch will ever be required, and this is always a plus. It is important to note that the American Kennel Club also has specific rules that must be followed when this method is used to produce a litter. Your Litter Registration Application form contains special instructions for the handling and processing of fresh, cooled, and frozen semen.

There is also the matter of proof that the semen you received is the semen that you requested. If you have any doubts about this, you might want to arrange to witness the stud's performance, the semen delivery, and/or the actual insemination itself. The best stand by for identification, would be DNA testing assuming you were alert enough to obtain a sample.

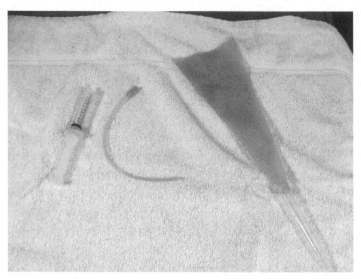

Artificial insemination tools from left to right.
Syringe for insemination, canine catheter, collection sheath and tube

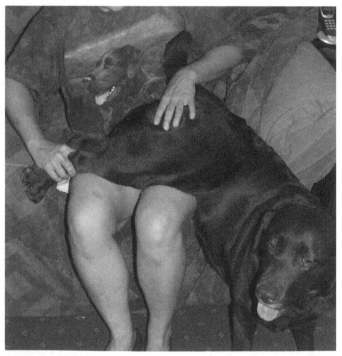

Bitch placement in order for her to receive the insemination.
Courtesy of Cedarbay labs.

Artificial insemination is starting to become the "breeding method of choice." Litter sizes use to be smaller compared to a traditional mating. Here is a litter of eight Cedarbay Chocolate Lab pups produced by artificial insemination. Eight pups is a good number for both an artificial and regular breeding.

Here is Penny after a recent breeding with Saddles.

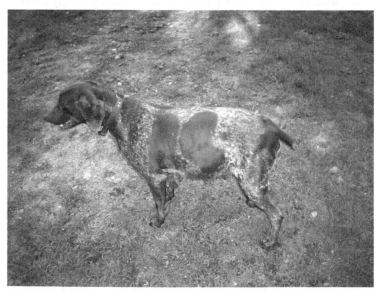

Here is Penny, sixty-three days later.
Photos by
Tom Dwyer

5

Maturation

Generally speaking, the success or failure of initiating a quality litter has been placed solely upon the stud dog inasmuch as he alone bears the siring burden. From that point on however, the stud bears very little responsibility for anything else. Interestingly enough, for the next five weeks, little or no help will be required from you either. Oh, you could probably have an ultrasound or x ray on the bitch. This will definitely confirm that she is going to have pups but not much more. I have learned from personal experience that neither procedure will guarantee you the exact count of live pups in the litter. An X ray I once had done, showed eight pups when there were actually nine and an ultrasound counted even fewer pups. In any event, there is very little constructive action you can take until she whelps. I will, of course, concede that weighing the cost of these medical procedures is your decision to make; nevertheless, from my prospective, unless these diagnostics are medically necessary, you will merely own some very expensive and highly unreliable pictures.

With the exception of keeping her confined until she is out of season, live life as you would prior to her mating. Time will pass quickly enough. Your dog will need exercise but try not to exhaust her. There are also a few things that you should know and do before whelping takes place.

GESTATION:

Sixty-three days is the average gestation periods for mated bitches—three days more or less depending on the bitch's age and the history of her gestation. Bitches who have whelped before are likely to go earlier while first time matings might take longer. It is also possible that you might have your bitch mated more than once and on different days.

Regardless, the gestation process starts on the first day of the mating, so, let's take a look at some important concerns.

1. Embryos will grow quickly over time but the first visible signs of pregnancy might not appear until about the fourth week. The teats should harden, although this also happens during false pregnancies—then gradually soften and enlarge. You might even have a change in pigmentation.

2. Food consumption will decrease at first but in time, she will be eating very heartily so, keep regular feeding schedules for the first month, followed by slightly increased feeding amounts starting from the 5th or 6th week and continue until whelping occurs.

Keeping her bowl full and nearby for when she wants it is nice, however, but try not to let her overeat. An overweight dog will crowd the pups and make whelping more difficult. Also, be advised that a food supplement will probably not be necessary. Canned dog food along with puppy dog food mixed into her regular feedings should contain enough nourishment for both mom and the pups.

3. This is also a good time to begin your record book. It should contain the history of both parents as well as a listing of the potential pups and to whom they will eventually be sold to. This stuff is important and, if you like, you may obtain preprinted forms for this purpose from the American Kennel Club. In order to streamline the process, be sure and get the Litter Registration Form which we mentioned earlier from the AKC. This should be filled out by both you and the stud owner, and with the only portion left un-entered should be the total number of live pups, male and female. Fill in that number and send it in to the AKC as soon as possible after the pups are born and they, in return, will send you individual puppy registration forms.

4. You'll need to prepare the whelping box. This should be done in an area that is quiet, and has ample room for your bitch to defecate. The whelping box should be constructed high enough off the ground to avoid drafts. Railings should also be added to prevent the mother from crowding her offspring. The sides of the box should be low enough for the mother to easily climb in an out, yet high enough to see that any drafts pass safely overhead. The box should also be long enough for the

mother to lie down and expose her teats for feeding. If you have previously used a whelping box before, then I would recommend changing the floor inasmuch as soiled wood retains the urine from previous litters.

Whelping boxes are designed to eliminate drafts so; this makes the use of fans counter productive. Think about it! If you need to use a fan to cool the mother, it is probably because you are overheating the surrounding area. Whelping boxes that are too hot will put too much stress on the bitch and aids in the dehydration of all the animals inside that box. This is not a good thing! It would be much wiser to reduce the ambient temperature rather than to bring in a fan. It is good to think of stuff like this beforehand. Lastly, the whelping box should be roomy enough to permit the growing pups to move about.

The use of heating pads inside of the whelping box is a nice thing, but I prefer to go one step further. I build my whelping boxes so that the heating pad goes under the box. This eliminates the electrical conduit from being exposed and a regular heating pad may be used rather than the more expensive interior units made especially for canine whelping boxes. It is also wise to set the heating pad on low. The wood under the box warms up nicely with this arrangement and then I am able to remove the pad after a couple days.

Start off with a simple floor base. Add a border around your base, about three or four inches high, to hold your railings.

Add another layer of wood on top of your border to create your railings. This will prevent the bitch from crowding the pups in the corners.

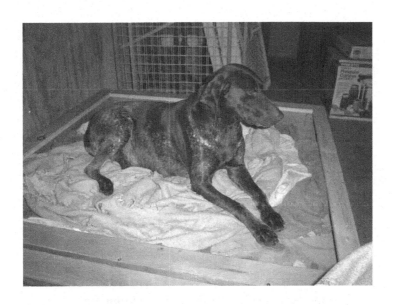

Be sure you give the whelping box a test run. Start by
having the expected mother spend as much time in it as
possible. Even while the whelping box is being built.

Adding height to the sides of the box is common as the pups get larger. This prevents them from escaping as they mature.

The size of the whelping box is determined by the size of the breed. Beagles, for example, do not need a four foot box like many of their larger cousins. A two foot box is more efficient and easier to handle.

A litter of Sunrise Beagle pups.
Photo by owner Robert C. Drozdowski

5. The number one puppy killer is chilling, so, it is critical to maintain as much body heat as possible immediately after birth. A heating system will likely be needed in the whelping area. Radiant heaters should not be used for this purpose—the only exception being the use of an oil filled radiant heater with an internal thermostat; otherwise, simply use your home heating system. Set the temperature between 75 and 85 degrees during the first two weeks after the litter is born. That, along with the heating pad placed under the whelping box, should be sufficient. The puppies will help the cause by bunching together for most of this time. Once everything is under control, you can reduce the temp to 72 to 80 and remove the heating pad.

Pups tend to huddle in the corners of the whelping box. Usually it is the warmest corner.

Puppies will stay within that general area even after the
heat is removed. They will do their doggie business on
one end of the box, and sleep at the other end.

Orphaned pups generally require 85 plus for heat. I personally lean toward 85 to 87 degrees. On the minus side, although, this temperature is still considered good for the litter, it will put a lot of strain on the Dam. She will pant and be extremely uncomfortable and it is possible that she might loose her milk early. These living conditions combined with the whelping process will in weigh heavily on the bitch's own ability to take care of herself. It has been said, "the stress will age the bitch" and when it is all said and done, your bitch might look very tired and much older looking, so, that light bulb on top of the whelping box that someone recommend . . . get rid of it. The room is supposed to be dimly lit and comfortable. Not very bright and hot.

6. Whether it is hay, or sawdust, the bedding should be padded. Newspapers and shredded newspaper will also do the job with the added benefit that they are absorbent and readily available.7. Be sure that the female is clean and free of parasites outside of her vaginal area as well as on her underbelly.

7. palpating or feeling for diagnostic purposes, is another process to be avoided. People are often frantic to see if they have some pups. You will know soon enough when she is going to drop a litter. Palpating, without knowing what you are doing, could severely damage or even destroy some pups during any stage of the pregnancy.

8. Move the expected mother into the whelping box about two weeks before whelping. This should be her permanent sleeping quarters until she whelps. Use only the bedding we recommended earlier. No pillows please.

9. You should have your whelping kit ready to go. Your kit should consist of some warm dry towels, sterile scissors, rectal thermometer, a hemostat (if you can get one), iodine solution, sewing thread (although I have never used it.), paper, pencil, water for the bitch, scale, emergency phone numbers, sterile surgical gloves, and a heating pad set for low. If you're keeping a portable or cellular phone nearby then I suggest you shut off the ringer. It's also a good idea to have a timepiece handy to measure the duration between deliveries.

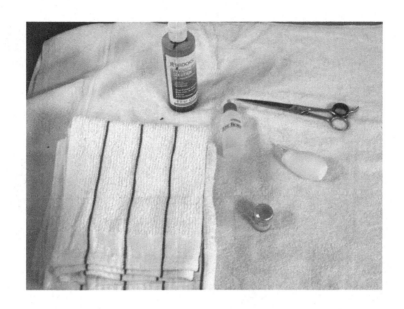

Here are some general whelping materials you will need.
Starting with the upper photo, we have towels, antiseptic
solution, nasal respirator, sterile scissors, and dental floss.
The lower photo consists of a heating pad, hemostats, rectal
thermometer, and s phone with the ringer off. Not pictured are some
sterile surgical gloves. Forget the scale. You will be too busy.

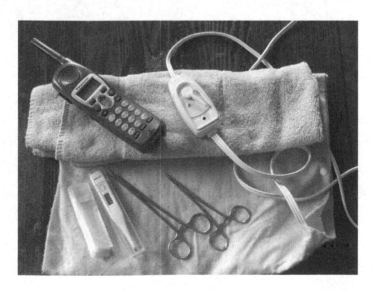

Ready?

6

Whelping

I sometimes dream in my mind's eye of a space age veterinary technology that would make it possible to place devices into a pregnant bitch and enable us to monitor and control the birthing process from conception through whelping. Indeed, it would be grand if we could control all of that stuff, but Mother Nature has (for eons) provide that any such intervention in her work would be merely meddlesome at best. So, allowing for the fact that embryonic growth and whelping are best handled by the dog herself, the breeder must be content to provide the secondary but equally important role of assisting in the delivery of healthy pups into a clean and supportive environment. In order to do this effectively, however, we must understand what to look for and how to deal with it. Let's first consider the birth process itself. Most bitches will, on average, whelp in about 63 days. Most will take 59 to 63 days, while first time mothers might take a little longer, about 64 to 67 days. Despite such uncontrollable variables, however, there are four consistent warning signs which will tip you off that she is about ready to deliver.

First, a visible mucus discharge will present itself. Pressure from inside the pup carrying horns will start to push mucus through the closed cervix. This discharge is more noticeable in the case of first time matings. Seasoned bitches, on the other hand, will clean themselves more often making discharge less apparent.

Second, her internal temperature should drop within forty-eight hours prior to whelping. This may or may not be accompanied by a noticeable discharge. In any event, things are now entering a new phase. The normal temperature for a dog is around 102 however, as delivery approaches, her temperature will go down to around 99 or less. This temperature decreases prior to whelping and is a natural process that chills the bitch and starts her contractions. It also means that she will most likely have pups *on the ground* within 24 hours of this temperature change. You must carefully monitor these temperature variations twice daily throughout the process with the use of a rectal thermometer. You should expect her temperature to return to normal near the end of delivery.

Third, as her uterus crowds, she will start cutting back on her food. She will eat smaller amounts but more frequently and when labor becomes imminent, she might stop eating altogether.

Fourth, her nesting instincts will change. If, for example, there are any newspapers in the whelping box, and she starts destroying them, shredding them, or pushing them about, you can be sure that birth is at hand. This activity may or may not be accompanied by panting.

Of all the indicators that we have examined, the best combination of barometers is mucus discharge followed by a temperature drop. If, at this point, you think you may need help; call your vet. If he is unavailable, the stud owner will probably be more than happy to assist you. Failing this, get hold of a knowledgeable friend or neighbor.

There are two important aspects related to temperature fluctuation that can indicate something is wrong. Temperature drops that remain low after labor could mean that the bitch is chilled and needs to be brought back to a stable internal reading of 102. I would exercise caution if you opt to use a heat lamp over her. Use it only for a short while and remove it as soon as the proper temperature is achieved. Conversely, be aware that an increase in temperature could also mean an infection is present and you should promptly notify your vet to obtain proper diagnosis and treatment. The most common cause for an increased temperature would be the retention of fetal material or placenta. This may be successfully treated with antibiotics.

The whelping process may vary anywhere from 15 minutes to one hour between puppies. Dams will usually have two horns. Each containing pups ready for delivery. One horn delivers at a time with a rest period before the other horn starts and the delivery begins all over again. Whatever pup is in line to be delivered, within that horn, will be next. There could be two or three pups from the same horn to be whelped before one pup from the other horn can be delivered. Anything over an hour between horns could mean the delivery is difficult and you should contact your vet for counsel. Granted, I have had litters whelp with as much as three hours between horns. I have even had a few stragglers come out the next morning. Novice or not, more than one hour between deliveries should put up the caution flag. If the dog starts to pant intermittently while straining her abdomen, it's time to get the whelping kit which you put together earlier in this book and role up your sleeves.

The bitch will start to destroy all the newspapers within the whelping box. This may or may not be accompanied by panting.

She will watch and clean her vaginal area as the first pup starts to appear.

Usually the sac containing the pup will emerge. Sometimes
the sac is already broken, and the pup comes out dry.

Just let things happen naturally. Help is usually not
needed. You may do more harm than good.

**Let the bitch clean up and inspect her new pup.
Congratulations, you have a litter "on the ground"
and the bitch is now called a "Dam".**

The most important thing you can do at this point is to remain calm. The first order of business will be to help nature take its course as quietly as possible. The water sac will be the first to appear. She might possibly need help with this but most of the time she will pass it alone. It is more likely that she will need help toward the end of the whelping when she is worn out. If this happens, gently grasp whichever part of the pup that has appeared, preferably the shoulders, and wait for the next contraction. So, when it comes, gently pull the pup toward the head of the bitch (never the tail) until the whole pup is out. The pup's natural exit will curve toward the head of the mother. Help the pup by pulling in precisely that direction. If you do this properly, the pup should slide right out. Remember, you should never pull on the pup when there is no contraction. In the first place, the pup won't move and in the second place, you could do more damage than good.

If the pup is still enclosed in the sac, tear open the sac which covers the head of the pup then pull gently on the umbilical cord to determine if the placenta is ready to come out. The placenta will not always come out after every pup. Sometimes two or three pups will exit before two or three placentas are expunged.

It is at this point that hernias are likely to happen. Abdominal hernias are the result of either fatty tissue or the intestinal tract penetrating through the abdominal wall at the exact spot where tension is placed at the umbilical cord. Too much tension creates a tear or a small hole. Imagine for a moment that you have a firm grip on the pup, and the bitch decides to move. It is entirely possible that reflectively, you might maintain your grip on the pup. If this happens, the cord will become taught. Hernia damage can also happen when, during birth, the pup is pressed down the horn so far and fast that the umbilical cord is placed under great strain. This is a time to be very patient. If she wants to push; let her push. You can best contribute by tearing open the sac while she chews on the cord. Conversely, if she wants to clean the pup then cut the cord while she cleans.

Let's assume, for a moment, that all goes well and the pups and mom are progressing nicely. When this happens, it is best to let things proceed naturally until she actually needs help. Once the puppy is out, tie off the umbilical cord with some thread (this is optional), clamp down on the cord about one inch from the stomach with a hemostat, then cut the cord. It is highly likely, however, that she will get the job done before you are able to react. While on the subject, I have never seen much blood from the wound after the cord has been cut. It dries up in no time and falls off within a couple days. On the other hand, extra naval string may just hinder the pup's mobility when searching for the teat.

I recommend that you only help the dam cut the cord when she is weak, tired, or multi-tasking by the cleaning of other pups. You can quickly do the job without much intervention into the mother's busy schedule. In any event, the dam will usually cut the cord. Once this is accomplished, place the pup with the head at your fingertips and the feet at your palms. If needed, put both hands together and, with a very slight downward motion, point the head of the pup to the floor then bring it back up. This technique will clean out the nasal area. Now, give the pup to the mother for cleaning. This is an optional procedure and is not needed if the pup is squeaking (puppy yelps) and actively moving about. Putting the pup back within the brood as soon as possible aids in both the cleaning of the puppy and it's bonding with mother. For first time whelpers, make sure you keep the pup low and show it to the mother so that she stays down. Help her dry the pup and make sure she knows that it is a good thing. This will help her stay in the box and might stop her from having the pups all over the place. At least one pup should always be with the mother because taking all the pups away could cause her contractions to stop. In the event that she is too tired, dry the pup yourself with a clean, dry cloth. If at any time, you discover pups sprawled all over the floor and delivered outside of the whelping box, scoop them up, dry them with "warm" towels, give them a minute on a heating pad, find the mother (who is probably with the rest of the brood) and put them under her. When you are sure that she is finished whelping, inspect and finish drying the rest litter and move them back to the whelping box at such a time as you let the Dam out to relieve her bladder. You might even have a chance to weigh a pup or two while she is out. Upon return, she should go directly to the box and inspect the litter. At this point I would caution you not let neighbors and relatives come and handle the pups. This should be avoided until the pups start weaning or their eyes open. A smart mother knows when someone touches her pups and excessive handling could make her reluctant too re-enter the whelping box as often as she should in order to nurse (if at all).

Umbilical hernias also occur when the bitch pulls the pup from the umbilical cord while she is cutting it. Pups sometimes are left to dangle in mid air while the mother trims off the cord. When this happens, get hold of the pup and raise it in order to reduce umbilical stress. Bring the pup down after she is finished and let mom finish her cleaning. Lastly, write down the time of delivery and a brief description of the dog on your note pad. Congratulations, she is now a dam.

It is also possible that your dog will probably want to eat the placenta. Whether or not she does, is up to you. Some will argue that it has no nutritional value while others insist that this tissue provides the dame with extra energy. Either way, this is too unimportant an issue to concern yourself with while you are scurrying about, cleaning and placing dogs back into the box while she is busy whelping. If she wants it then let her have it, and keep yourself focused on the more important stuff. Meanwhile, the dam might not let her pups feed until she has delivered all of them, so, don't be surprised if she keeps them close at hand until the last one is out.

In truth, it may or may not be necessary for you to do any of the exercises that we have just reviewed. All you might need is a good book and a comfortable chair; nevertheless, it is good to be prepared.

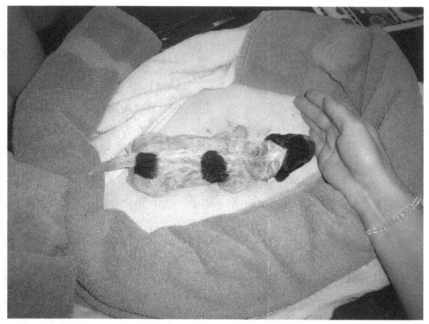

Keep the heating pad on low. Roll up another towel to form a barricade.
Dry off and inspect the pup. Then return it back to his mother.

Photo By
Tom Dwyer

Having the pup suckle will keep the contractions
coming at regular intervals.

After the pups are born, the dame's uterus will continue to contract as it returns to its normal size; nevertheless, her milk will be ready long before that happens and it is essential for the pups to begin feeding soon. Colostrum, which provides the puppies with valuable antibodies, is available in the mother's milk for only about 24 hours. So, of the pup can't find his mother, it is critical to make certain that she finds him.

UTERINE INERTIA:

It is appropriate at this point, to discuss the phenomenon known as uterine inertia. As I noted earlier, if the bitch continues to push with no results for hours on end, it is time to call your vet. Uterine inertia occurs primarily in whelping bitches, who are near the end of their delivery, bitches who are too tired to continue, older dogs, or dogs who were not good candidates for breeding in the first place. In any event, bitches that have had exhaustive deliveries, will, "poop out" so to speak. This is called uterine inertia. It can also happen when all the pups are born and the dam has no strength to push out all the nasty leftovers from inside herself.

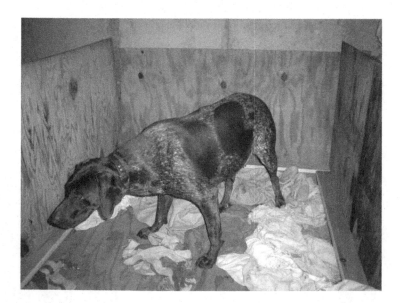

A pit shot, (Oxytocin), may be injected into the bitch to enhance contractions. It is used for overweight dogs and out of shape dogs, and dogs that have been mated many times. Females such as these often become distended to the point where they couldn't push out a pup no matter how hard they tried. As a result, placenta and other associated material stays in the horns, and the Dam is likely to get a uterine infection which will contaminate her milk. If this happens, you will have to treat your dog's symptoms and feed the pups yourself, but the pups still have to come out and a pit shot usually will restart her contractions in the uterus. If the Oxytocin fails, then the caesarian section is your last resort, however, you will never have this problem if the dam is in good physical condition. To date, I have never found it necessary to use a pit shot.

FETAL DISTRESS:

Fetal distress will usually go hand in hand with Uterine Inertia. Fetal distress occurs when labor puts a heavy strain on the whelping bitch. The best way to tell if she is in distress is to put on your sterile surgical gloves, located in your puppy whelping kit, and place one or two fingers in the vaginal area to see if you can locate and estimate how far the pup is in the canal. It is important to notice the color of the discharge on your gloves upon their removal. Green is a bad color because it means that she is becoming distressed. Continue whelping if a pup is discharged after the removal of your fingers but call your vet if she continues to strain after a short while. Time is of the essence at this point, so do not dally. Your vet will give you the option of a Caesarian, or an injection of Oxytocin. In the event that Oxytocin doesn't do the job, act quickly. Pups are waiting to come out *now* and a Caesarian will deliver more of them, faster and alive.

NEARING THE END:

See to it that the dame is let out to relieve herself as often as required, but go with her in case she drops another pup while outside. Also, have plenty of water and food available for when she gets hungry again. If she doesn't want her regular dry food, then mix some canned food in with it. Some would argue that this might not be good for her digestive tract but I strongly prefer to see a mother with a full stomach; ready to feed her pups.

If the puppies sleep soundly after eating, it means that they are getting enough nourishment and all is well. This is a good time to change the bedding in the whelping box and to start weighing the puppies. Document each pup's weight to reference their weight increases.

So that you don't go into shock, be advised that the mother eats the poop. It's O.K. She'll stop when they get older, but for now it is her job to clean it up. The mother also has to stimulate the pup's bladder to urinate. It is the only way to clean their plumbing. You can help her by stroking the pup's area of urination with a warm moist cloth. They will be ready to go after a few caresses.

Contact your vet and share any questions or concerns that you may have with him. He may elect to see the mother and her new brood if one of your issues alarms him. If not, he will offer his congratulations.

Keep the room containing the whelping box dimly lit and quiet. You need only enter periodically to let the dame outside and check on the pups. Other than that, the next four weeks will be pretty much a waiting period, during which you will not have much to do except observe and maintain whelping box hygiene. The new mother, on the other hand, will be kept busy cleaning and feeding her pups a half dozen times a day. If she's lucky, she might even get in a little sleep.

You also have to check the mother before the big day ends. Do this by placing your hands up onto the abdomen and palpate to see if all the pups have been delivered. Any lumps could be another pup and this means that she is not through delivering yet. Trust me—if they are in there, you will feel them. This happens fairly often so don't be surprised when she delivers again. This occurs because while the pups are feeding on mom's teats, the suckling and paw scratching creates contractions in the uterus. This in turn pushes out all the excess from delivery. Everything will come out, including the last pup—dead or alive. Any pieces that come out afterwards and during delivery are dead pups that were being absorbed. The contracting uterus is cleaning out the system. This is why the ghost stories about mummified pups are just that—*stories*.

Finally, any lump discovered in a bitch during an examination prior to her eventual breeding, would be considered timorous. Such a finding is extremely suspicious and the dog should not be allowed to have been mated to begin with.

**Photos
By
Jane Dwyer**

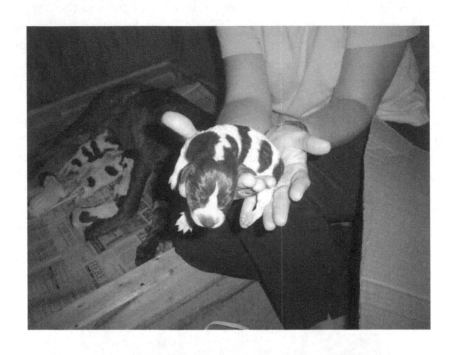

7

Puppy Care

Survival within a litter is often problematic. Every once and a while, it may become necessary to separate a puppy from his litter mates and in extreme cases, you might even have to put a puppy down. There is also the ominous possibility that you might find a pup who has already expired while under your care. Given these scenarios, it behooves you to keep an eye on the natural growth and development of each pup as well as his siblings. In order to do that, it will be most helpful to anticipate the range of crises that stand in the way of proper growth and development. They are, in no particular order:

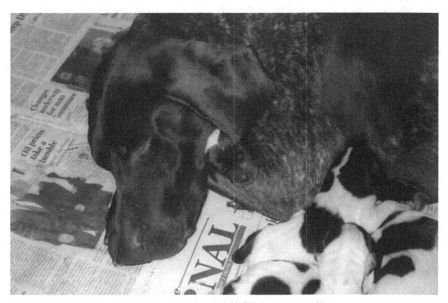

**Looking closely, you will find one small pup,
resting comfortably, under the dam's ear.**

CHILLED PUPS:

The normal temperature of a dog is around 101.2 Fahrenheit. As we noted in chapter 6, expecting mothers reduce their body temperature to around 99 degrees before they whelp. This means of course, that all of the puppies temperatures are the same as the Dam's during whelping. What happens next is that whelped pups with reduced temperatures are suddenly thrust into a room whose temperature is even lower.

A warm pup always has warm (pink or light red) paws. This means that their blood is circulating properly and even though the paws and nose might seem a little cold, as long as they are pink, the pups are doing well and just need to be snuggled closer to mom. Therefore, pups whelped under normal conditions will naturally gravitate toward their mother for both food and warmth. The continuous arranging and rearranging of the nestled pups help the circulation of blood flow and although the paws may feel cold, pink is more important. Blue, on the other hand, is not a good color and any puppy that seems to be colder than the rest might be chilled. This problem requires immediate attention. Once a puppy becomes chilled, it is nearly impossible for him to raise his body temperature by himself and his chances for survival may be slim. You should immediately remove the puppy from the litter and line a small heating pad with a couple of towels, set for low, and wrap the assembly completely around the pup. Insert a thermometer inside to monitor the temperature and if his body temperature stabilizes, open up the heating pad and wrap another towel around the pup so as to form a donut. Be aware, however, him fully wrapped will dehydrate him; hence, the chimney effect from the donut will vent any excess heat away. At this point, try returning him to the litter and see if mom will let him be cleaned and suckle; if not, he will require supplemental feeding before he is returned again. In either case, consult with your veterinarian. You might have an orphaned pup on your hands.

CRUSHED PUPS:

It is a sad fact that the number one killer of pups in the early stages of life is chilling. It is equally unfortunate that inadvertent crushing by protective mothers is the number one killers of pups who have survived the chilling stage.

Although the crushing of pups can occur at any time, it is most likely to occur after their internal temperature becomes stable and before their eyes are fully opened. It can happen very quickly and without notice, and if you are not quick at hand, you stand too loose a perfectly healthy puppy.

The mother, being the caring Dam that she is, will clean the pups while they nurse. Cleaning those who are readily accessible is easy. The ones farther down the feeding line are more difficult inasmuch as she has to reach farther down to complete her task. To do this, she must push herself up, then, reach down as far as she can, to the last nursing teat on her body. This raises her front end, and while she is in this position, the pups who are in the front now can move so far down the front so much that they can actually nurse from the mother's lower side. Tragedy strikes when mom finishes her cleaning duties, returns down to her natural nursing position, and crushes the exposed front pup.

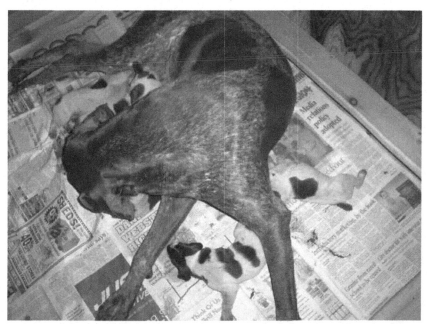

Here you find the dam cleaning her pups while one suckles the top teat on the other side.

Once again, you will see the dam cleaning her pups
while another is feeding below her left leg.
Crushing the pup is almost imminent.

The dam will usually start separating the pups into groups. This
reduces the amount of confusion and creates for better management.

If you have to intervene, then I would recommend having the
dam leave the box all together for feedings. Returning only
the pups when feedings and cleanings are complete.

Photo by
Tom Dwyer

**Photo of Robert with Sunrise Spice's Raisins &
her litter of pups feeding on a coat.
Photo by Kim C. Drozdowski**

WEAK OR SICK PUPPIES:

So, there you have it. Some pups will die due to chilling, while others pups will be crushed during nursing. These tragedies are likely to happen unless you keep a 24-hour vigil and more problems will also surface in the weeks ahead.

Within a few days you may notice that one or more of the litter appears weak or is acting timidly toward his siblings. You might even see the mother pushing away a pup from the feeding area—refusing to nurse it. This is sometimes caused by the pup's cold or chilled nose. The mother naturally reacts to this cold nose by pushing the young pup aside.

In other situations, some pups lack the ability to ingest food from either his mothers teats, or from supplemental feedings. This condition in a young pup is commonly caused by two situations: either the young pups have not acquired the ability to suckle, or he is simply too weak to latch onto the teat and pull. Both dilemmas usually go hand in hand and are easily recognized by comparing the feeding habits of all of the pups within the litter.

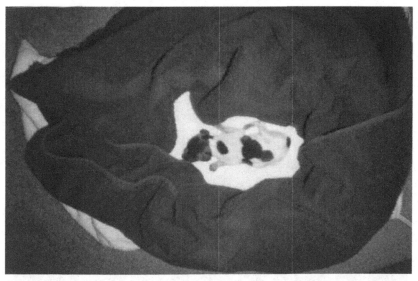

Heating pads are to be set on low for sick and orphaned pups.

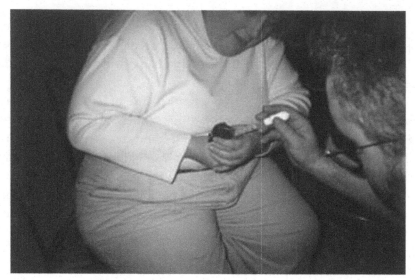

Kim Leeman with breeder trying to encourage suckling when attempting to feed.

This will help as the dog ages and the bottle size increases.

Lack of nourishment along with rough house games are common realities among puppies and any member of the litter who can't deal with this, may have to be removed from the litter for his own safety. Any such undernourished pups must be given a separate teat or be bottle fed. It's uncommon for puppies, so isolated, to become seriously injured or even accidentally killed, but it still happens. So, it's a good idea to watch the animals closely for any changes in their condition and contact your vet if you suspect anything is wrong.

**Try and return the pup to the litter box as soon as possible.
Monitor aggression and be sure that she is well socialized.
Remove her, if she can't handle her litter mates.**

EYES:

After about 10 to 14 days, the pups will start to open their eyes. At this time, their eyes are extremely sensitive to strong light, so, in order to prevent serious damage, maintain a low lighting level in the room. Also, at this time, you will begin to notice subtle personality or behavioral quirks in most of the puppies. Some, for example, may remain close to mom while others will regularly climb on top of the pile to sleep. These same traits will magnify as the pup grows older and will help you to evaluate the entire litter. Sharing these traits with potential buyers will aid in their selection process. In some cases, the extra cautious buyer will request an evaluation certificate. This means that the breeder will call in an outside *expert* to roll a can or squeak a toy in order to evaluate a particular pup's personality. It seems odd to me that a stranger, who has never seen your litter would be better qualified to evaluate the pups you have been tending to for eight weeks—but there you have it.

Shortly after they open their eyes, the puppies will begin to struggle with their first steps. When they are about two and one half to three weeks old, you should start weaning them.

WEANING:

The main challenge during weaning is to find a way to release your pups from the suckling of mom's teats, and get them to acquire a taste for kibble. Weaning consists of two separate stages. The first is best achieved by bringing the little pups something sweet and yummy. This is only a short term fix that takes about two weeks. During this process, the mother will still be actively feeding the litter. The second challenge is the actual physical separation between mother and pup's. This process will take about four weeks.

The development of the pup's milk teeth is a sure sign that it is time for weaning to begin and, should you fail to recognize this signal, mom will tend to matters herself by forcing the pups away soon as she feels the pain of a dozen teeth on her nipples.

Everyone seems to have their own special gruel formula to use while weaning the puppies away from their mother and I'm no different. Although most formulas contain different mix ratios, they all have the same nutrients. For example, I use condensed milk mixed with baby formula, puppy formula, warm water, and some finely ground puppy food which I run through a coffee grinder. Starting with small amounts, I gradually add enough ground food to the water so as to loosely hold the solution together to form a soup, however, this mixture can still be a bit too crunchy for the pups, so I usually also let it set for a while until it becomes soggy. I will then add some baby formula and condensed milk.

You should wait until the dame has left the box for whatever reason before placing a bowl of the food mixture into the box—preferably in a spot that the puppies have not soiled. Then pick up a pup and dip his nose slightly in the bowl and let him lap the food from his face. He will probably begin eating from the bowl immediately. Repeat this process with all of his siblings once a day, gradually adding more and more puppy food to the mix and reducing the amount of condensed milk each time. By the end of the fourth week, the final product should be soft puppy food accompanied by warm water. Try not to use the water in the gruel formula at room temperature or colder least the pups will become cold internally and start to shake. Keep a bowel of water at room temperature, and some dry crushed puppy food on the side for them to pick on when they are ready. You will soon be able to leave dry, non crushed food and a separate water bowel for their dining pleasure.

Some members of the litter may need a second or third introduction to the bowl but in time, they will all be fighting for a corner of the dish. The bowl to be used should be a basic stainless steel puppy feeding dish, round and raised in the center. This configuration allows the pups to feed while preventing any one pup from standing in the middle. In spite of this design, it is still surprising to see at least one standing in the middle.

The pups should be completely weaned by four to five weeks of age. Mother's milk is still the best, however, so, let her go back into the box if she so desires. Be sure and leave water in the box for the puppies. It probably won't remain upright for very long, but they will need something to drink when awake.

The development of the pup's milk teeth is a sure sign that it is time for weaning to begin. Should you fail to recognize this signal, mom will tend to the matter herself. She will force the pups away as soon as she feels the pain of a dozen teeth on her nipples.

Pick up a pup and dip his nose slightly in the bowl and let him lap the food from his face. He will probably begin eating from the bowl immediately. Repeat this process with all of his siblings once a day.

By the end of the fourth week, the final product should be soft puppy food accompanied by warm water.

Gradually add more puppy food and start thinning out the formula, as the pups increase in size. With the final product being kibble and water.

Unfortunately, they do not have any table manners!

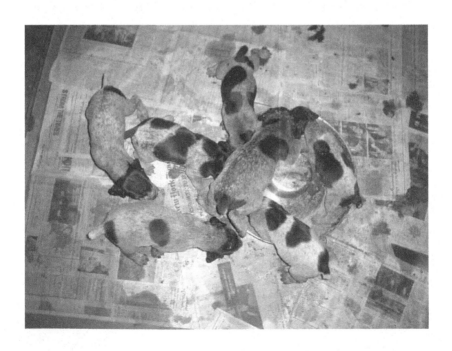

The next problem is to stop the dame from producing milk and, in order to accomplish this, I use a time-tested method. I give her exactly one quarter of her food intake for one day or twenty-four hour period and about half her daily intake for the next feeding. I complete the change in feeding pattern with three-quarters on the third day and a full portion on the fourth. The portions of food that she is to receive are that what she normally ate before she was bred. This temporary food restriction, coupled with her no longer feeding pups, will stop her from producing milk. There might be excessive caking on her teats during this stage; hence, any reduction of this caking is a good sign that everything is working.

BLOAT/BLOCKAGE:

Puppy bloat is easy to explain but difficult to describe. Put simply, a bloated pup is a dog that has eaten too much. This problem often occurs in orphaned pups who have eaten beyond their ability to digest. It can also be attributed to the large amount of air which is ingested when they gobble down their food. It is also possible that there might be a blockage in the digestive track, preventing food from passing through. In order to identify a bloated animal, turn the pup on his backside and tap his stomach. If this pup is indeed bloated, a tight drum sound will emanate from the distended stomach. The best thing to do at this point, would be to monitor the amount of food he consumes in one single feeding. If bloating continues, two things might help alleviate the symptoms.

A. Stimulate excretion by wiping the anal and urinary area with a warm moist cloth. Do this with a gentle motion until excretion occurs. If this doesn't work, go to step B.

B. If the stimulation only results with urine, then it's time to apply some mineral oil in two places. A small amount should be given both orally and naturally (novices, consult your vet for recommended dosages).

If remedies A and B don't work then bloat may not be the problem. Your pup probably needs to be wormed.

WORMING:

Worm the pup with a soft worming product which contains the active ingredient *Pyrentle*. The product acts more like a worm laxative, is better for pups, and is harder to overdose than *Pepperzine*. Which acts more like a worm poison, and is a lot stronger for killing the worms in pups; consequently, many breeders choose to use *Pyrentle*.

Your first or second worming will result in an avalanche of worms. A very small amount of blood might also be evident. Continue with the worming, follow the directions and all will soon be well.

DIARRHEA:

This is not a good thing to occur at any stage of a dog's life. Greenish-yellow and watery stools lead to dehydration and should be dealt with as soon as possible. My experience has been that diarrhea will happen in three stages during the pups first eight weeks of life. It comes from:

1. Soiled whelping boxes. Papers have not been changed regularly and the bitch's teats have been severely compromised. This type of infection is the result of poor sanitation.
2. The weaning of a pup from mothers milk to puppy gruel and from gruel to dry kibble. This is a normal reaction to food change.
3. Worms, or the worming process.

My choice of treatment is Kaopectate or a generic version of it. Again, as in the case of mineral oil, it is recommended that first time or inexperienced breeders contact their vet for proper dosages.

Personally, I prefer to use half the dosages as they relate to the Pyrentle I use for worming. For example, if I were using 5cc for every 5 pounds of Pyrentle, then my dosage for Kaopectate would be 2.5 cc per 5 pounds.

Be advised that Kaopectate works fast and one dose is usually all you will need to eliminate the runs. Another word of caution—remember that the pup's digestive system is still underdeveloped and sensitive; consequently, this treatment should be used sparingly and cautiously.

ACIDOPHILOUS:

Diarrhea and constipation can sometimes occur while in the middle of weaning from mothers' milk to solid foods. This is probably due to the loss of a naturally occurring bacterium, which is found in the pup's intestinal tract. Although this distress can be resulted from the bacteria alone, it may become necessary to chemically jump start the whole process by helping Mother Nature along with a *propionic bacterium* called acidophilous.

Acidophilous, which occurs naturally in fermented dairy products such as yogurt, serves to rejuvenate the pup's natural antibodies and strengthen his immune system. This, in turn, will counteract his constipation and allow for more normal bowel movements. Conversely, diarrhea problems should clear up quickly if the bacterium was absent in the pup's system. Acidophilous may be found refrigerated, in any health food store. I recommend using the powdered form inasmuch as you will better able to control the proper dosage by sprinkling it onto the puppy food.

Another word of caution—if you are going to continue this practice, remember that a dog's meal should always be balanced. Introducing an additive to his food is justified only if and when he needs the extra supplement. The random or arbitrary addition of vitamin supplement agents such as those found in dairy products, could lead to serious joint problems like Hypertrophic Osteodystrophy which we discussed earlier.

CALCIUM:

If you haven't already noticed, I tend to revisit the notion of proper calcium dosages throughout this book. In the earliest part of the dog's life, particularly during the weaning process, we as owners, play a vital role not only in the growing dog's development but in his well being as an adult also. It follows that the dog's diet is critical to his or her development. *What* you feed him, as well as *how* you feed you're pup will influence the management of his health throughout his life.

Believe it or not, most dog foods on the market today have enough daily recommended nourishment to sustain your dog for as long as he lives. The key here is that most dog foods are *already* balanced as far as their nutritional content is concerned and this balance accounts for most of the important vitamin and mineral additives. This balance is also designed so as not to have more than what is needed of any specific element; inasmuch as this can disrupt the balance of other vitamins or minerals.

Specifically, let's consider the use of the minerals Calcium, Zinc, and Phosphorus. Too much Zinc can cause a deficiency in both Phosphorous and Calcium. Too much Calcium can cause a Phosphorous deficiency as well as problems with bone growth. On the other hand, too much prosperous will result in a calcium deficiency that, in turn, generates a whole new set of bone growth irregularities.

Clearly then, giving your dog large amounts of unnecessary supplements will, in the long run, cause more bone problems than it will solve. Supplements should be given only to dogs who need them—amen! Remember also that supplements are directly linked to your puppy's weaning period so, once he is fully weaned on puppy kibble; keep him there until he is ready for adult dog food.

ADULT DOG FOOD:

Personally, I do not keep my dogs on puppy food any longer than about eight months of age. At that time, I will take a fifty-pound bag of his puppy food and fifty pounds of what he will be eating for the rest of his life and mix the two. He will eventually be free to eat regular food once your one hundred-pound supply mix is gone and, you guessed right—that will take a long time.

Marianne Rousseau showing us her expanded whelping box
Photo by
Tom Dwyer

OPENING THE WHELPING BOX:

Whelping boxes should be designed so that it is easy for the puppies to get in and out of them. Not only will this help with the muscle development of the pups, but it will automatically create separate eating and excretions areas outside the whelping box. This has the additional sanitary benefit of limiting the box to serve as sleeping quarters only.

The initial box, is initially intended to contain the pups along with the dam until the pups start the process of weaning, then, I lower the front of the box, giving the pups the option to come and go as they please. To get them to leave, I place a bowl of puppy gruel outside of the whelping box as bait. Of course, they take the bait and spend much of their time sniffing, peeing and playing. I sometimes find it necessary, however, to pick up any pups who are reluctant to leave the box and set them down outside. Funny, they all seem to know enough to return to the box when they want to sleep. Before you know it, they are all pooping and eating outside and sleeping inside. This is a great first step for early puppy behavioral evaluations.

Whelping boxes should be expanded to encourage the pups to distinguish their eating, sleeping, and playing areas.

Expanding the whelping box greatly improves the initial social
habits of your litter. The box still has to be cleaned and managed
to prevent infections. Exercise is also a must. Therefore, we
should still introduce them to the great out doors.

Urinary Track Infections:

Although the bitch tries hard to keep her pups clean, most whelping boxes still contain some degree of soil. Whelping boxes with wood bottoms are great for traction when compared to laminated bottoms, however, wood bottoms tend to absorb excrement from the pups and as a result, urinary tract infections may surface within the litter. Pups who are infected, often seem to be a little less aggressive and may even distance themselves form the other pups. Their disposition has been compromised by their illness and their behavior is often mistakenly seen as timid. The treatment is simple and a visit to your vet for some antibiotics should solve the problem. In addition, I would strongly suggest that you change the wood floor of your whelping box if you are planning to use it again in the future.

While social habits start from within the whelping box. They
are escalated when they are free to run and explore.
Start them off in an enclosed area where they
can explore their new surroundings.

They will soon find their own gathering place where they
can explore and socialize till their hearts content.

They will soon be eating, exploring and burning
up much needed puppy calories.

Best of all, it will give them much needed naps.
All this is being done while you clean up and sterilize the whelping area.

Limping Pups:

At the risk of belaboring the obvious, puppies play hard and their horseplay can be so intense as to leave them limping. A limp is not always just a limp; however, it is good to distinguish between the two types for the sake of proper treatment. The most simple, paw raising limps, will heal with time, but three-legged limps will take much longer to resolve themselves.

The common paw raising limp usually goes unnoticed when the pup is running or playing; nevertheless, it becomes quite apparent when he walks. So, check his paws to verify that there are no cuts, puncture wounds, or cracked and broken nails. Any of these injuries can be treated quickly and, if severe enough, might require a call to the vet. On the other hand, no visible injuries could mean an internal problem which will need time to heal. If the limp continues, reduce his play time, remove him from his litter mates, and call your vet for his opinion.

A three-legged limp is a more severe problem. The dog can neither walk nor run on the injured leg. If his limp is accompanied by a whimper or yelp, he will need immediate attention. Starting with the paw, check for the usual damage such as, the nails, and cut paws. Also, check the foot, joints, and legs by giving a slight squeeze in each area of the leg while observing for reactions such as a slight tug/or whimper. Recognizing where the injury is does not mean that you can treat it however, and it's now time to call your vet for treatment options

Be on guard, however, if pain killers are the treatment of choice for they tend to mask the basic problem. As I mentioned in Chapter 3, dog's natural reaction to an injured leg is to raise it because he relies on the pain to tell him how much pressure he may put on the injured leg. Accordingly, more pressure will be put on the leg if the pain subsides. The use of pain killers eliminates the animal's natural ability to distinguish if he is injured or not; hence, he places more pressure on the injured area which can increase the injury and delay the healing process.

If you and your vet determine that his injury is not that severe, (something that does not require surgery) then I would recommend reducing the pup's activity for a while. The pup will let you know if he is healing or not through his activities and actions. Nature is often the best healer.

SWIMMERS

I always experience a great sense of satisfaction and relief when the entire litter has finally learned how to stand up. Once in a while, however, I find a pup that is still unable to use his hind legs to pull himself up. This condition is every bit as serious as low body temperature. I call these little guys' *swimmers* and always remove them from the litter immediately.

Chances are that the puppy is the victim of slippery linoleum or wood floors inside of the whelping box. The trick is to get him onto a rough surface such as carpeting or (weather permitting) grass. He may continue to struggle for as long as a week but eventually, he should be able to stand correctly on his own. Once this happens, you may safely return him to the litter.

In the event he can't recover, you probably pulled him out of the box too late and his legs are already beginning to grow out of their sockets. If this condition is not promptly treated, the animal will become permanently disabled and will probably need to be euthanized. Many breeders and vets give up at this point, but I have one last trick up my sleeve. With the help of a very good veterinarian, I force the dog's legs back into a normal position. This does not hurt him. Then, I apply tape just above the pads of the hind feet and tape the hind legs together; leaving a three finger wide space between the legs.

Exercise is the next concern and your pup will likely continue to struggle with the task of standing, so I periodically stand him up and help him to balance himself. The rest of the time, I just wait and observe. If he cannot manage after eight weeks, you will probably have to put him down. Remember, however, that he does not have to be walking. He just has to be able to *get up*. Once he does this, he will have cleared the most critical hurdle. In the event that he is able to stand, leave the tape on until he can walk on all four legs with reasonable ease.

I have successfully used this method on a dog-named Buddy Buoy at a time when many others had written him off. I hope some of them are reading this chapter. Don't thank me—thank my vet.

PINK EYE:

Conjunctivitis, or Pink Eye, as it is more commonly called, is a very common ailment with puppies and older dogs alike. It is the irritation of the tissue lining the eyelids near the cornea. This irritation is usually due to allergies such as pollen or grass and, in some cases, is caused by viruses or bacteria.

Pink Eye will often clear up as fast as it originated, usually, however, it must be treated with drops or ointments. More severe cases such as ulcerations in the eye will be medicated differently. In any event, your veterinarian will be the best judge of diagnosis and treatment.

**You have done a great job raising your litter
to the ripe old age of eight weeks.**

**It is now time for these pups to bask in the affection of others.
Here, Fred Newcomb enjoys the comfort of this loveable pup.**

Sarah Saunders is surprised to find that these pups have never seen a sandal before. Retrieving the sandal proved to be a challenge.

Fred Newcomb Jr. enjoying the socialization of one very relaxed yet curious puppy.

Eventually, you will have to sell your pups. You can't keep them all! Here,
Miss Elle starts on her journey home with new owner Dale Banfield.
Photo by
Tom Dwyer

FINAL THOUGHTS:

Hopefully, this book has helped you think through some of the rough
but necessary steps required to breed, whelp, and nurse your litter of pups.
The degree to which you follow the guidance I have provided is entirely
up to you.

Many breeding topics such as tail and ear docking are *breed specific* and
as such, require patience and training. So, unless you have the stomach to
remove of your pups dew claws, it might be better to leave these things to
your vet.

This book is not a one size fits all solution, however, it is likely that
you will find it necessary to groom my methodology to fit your particular
situation. With that said, the only other advice that I can offer, to ensure a
safe and long-lived relationship with your canine is as follows.

1. Please watch your dog's food intake after puppyhood.
2. Never over vaccinate your puppy.
3. Keep grooming up to date.
4. Use low amounts of soap when giving puppy baths.
5. Muscle development is essential.
6. Crates should only be used for sleeping and travel.
7. Never stress him to the point of fear.
8. Breed for intelligence.

Most things can be achieved in the simplest manner with the easiest solutions to the most complex problems. Modern science along with solid old fashion values is the key to breeding quality dogs. I hope you enjoyed this book as much as I did putting it together.

Enjoy your dog!

A Special Thanks to

Tal Allen and Thor

David, Tracy & Dale Banfield and Miss Elle

Kim & Robert Drozdowski and Sunrise Beagles

My support team, Jane, Evan Lyndsey & LeAnna Dwyer

Thomas F. Dwyer

Dave Hebert and Blaze & Roxie

Chris Holiday and Sydney

Kim Leeman

Midwestern Pet Foods and Pro Pac

Michele McKechnie & Brent Stechowitch and Nicki

Fred Newcomb Jr.

Pat Russell, Fred Newcomb and Birdland Kennels

Lee & Wayne Robinson and Robi Read & White Setters

Marianne L. Rousseau and Cedarbay Kennels

Sara Saunders

Tom White With his Spotted Hill GSP's